Somalia: State Collapse and the Threat of Terrorism

Ken Menkhaus

ADELPHI PAPER 364

Oxford University Press, Great Clarendon Street, Oxford OX2 6DP
Oxford New York

Athens Auckland Bangkok Bombay Calcutta Cape Town
Dar es Salaam Delhi Florence Hong Kong Istanbul Karachi
Kuala Lumpur Madras Madrid Melbourne Mexico City Nairobi
Paris Taipei Tokyo Toronto
and associated companies in Ibadan

Oxford is a trade mark of Oxford University Press

Published in the United States
by Oxford University Press Inc., New York

© The International Institute for Strategic Studies 2004

First published March 2004 by **Oxford University Press** for
The International Institute for Strategic Studies
Arundel House, 13–15 Arundel Street, Temple Place, London WC2R 3DX
www.iiss.org

Director John Chipman
Editor Tim Huxley
Copy Editor Matthew Foley
Production Simon Nevitt

British Library Cataloguing in Publication Data
Data available

Library of Congress Cataloguing in Publication Data

ISBN 0-19-851670-3
ISSN 0567-932X

Contents

Maps and Tables

Glossary

AIAI	Al-Ittihad al-Islamiyya
AMREF	African Medical and Research Foundation
CSIS	Center for Strategic and International Studies
DoD	US Department of Defense
DoS	US Department of State
ICG	International Crisis Group
IDP	Internally displaced persons
IGAD	Intergovernmental Authority on Development
JVA	Jubba Valley Alliance
NGO	Non-governmental organisation
NSC	National Salvation Council
SNA	Somali National Alliance
SNM	Somali National Movement
SPM	Somali Patriotic Movement
SRRC	Somali Reconciliation and Restoration Council
SSDF	Somali Salvation Democratic Front
RRA	Rahanweyn Resistance Army
TNG	Transitional National Government
UN	United Nations
UNICEF	United Nations Children's Fund
UNOSOM	United Nations Operation in Somalia
USC	United Somali Congress
VHF	Very High Frequency (radio)

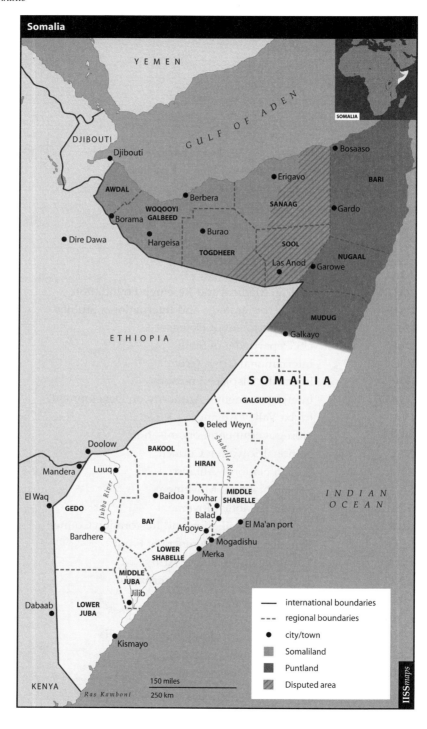

Somalia

Introduction

Protracted state collapse has bedevilled the best humanitarian, diplomatic, development and peacekeeping efforts of the international community. Prior to 11 September 2001, external engagement in crises such as those in northern Iraq, Somalia, Rwanda, Bosnia and Haiti tended to be driven more by humanitarian and political pressures – the need to be seen to 'do something' about a wrenching tragedy given saturation media coverage – than by national-security imperatives.[1] Collapsed states have routinely been characterised as a threat to international peace and security, particularly in UN Security Council resolutions authorising peacekeeping missions.[2] But this has portrayed collapsed states as threats to international security in the broadest sense of the word – as breeding-grounds for disease, refugee flows, arms-trafficking, transnational crime, environmental destruction, regional instability and other problems. Throughout the 1990s, arguments promoting the 'securitisation' of complex emergencies – whether advanced by humanitarian lobbyists trying to generate greater international engagement, or by security analysts genuinely concerned at the threats these zones of state collapse might pose – were at best a partial success.[3] Decisions to engage with or ignore collapsed states were driven mainly by political, not strategic, calculations.

This changed dramatically in the wake of the terrorist attacks of 11 September. Since then, collapsed states have commanded new attention as potential safe havens for transnational terrorist groups. A study by the Association of the US Army and the Center for Strategic and International Studies (CSIS) in 2002 sums up the new zeitgeist:

> *One of the principal lessons of the events of September 11 is that failed states matter – not just for humanitarian reasons but also for national security as well. If left unattended, such states can become sanctuaries for terrorist networks with a global reach, not to mention international organized crime and drug traffickers who also exploit the dysfunctional environment. As such, failed states can pose a direct threat to the national interests of the United States and to the stability of entire regions.[4]*

But elevated concern about collapsed states as a threat to international peace and security has yet to translate into more effective strategies and tools to address them. They remain one of the most enduring foreign-policy frustrations of the post-Cold War era, as experience in Afghanistan and Iraq since 2001 makes clear.

Nowhere has the crisis of state collapse been as profound and prolonged – and as misunderstood – as in Somalia, which has gone without any functioning central government since January 1991. Numerous external attempts have been made to revive a central state; all have failed. In 1993–95, the UN Operation in Somalia (UNOSOM), one of the most expensive and ambitious peace-enforcement operations ever launched by the international community, was derailed by armed conflict and never came close to pulling together a working national administration. Between 1991 and 1999, more than a dozen internationally sponsored national reconciliation conferences were held on Somalia, none of which produced a lasting accord. In 2000, another external mediation effort was undertaken, this time by the government of Djibouti, with the strong support of the UN. These talks, known as the Arta process, produced a Transitional National Government (TNG) in August 2000. The TNG received recognition at the UN and garnered an estimated $50 million in aid from Arab Gulf states, but was never able to assume control over more than a portion of the capital, Mogadishu. By 2002 the TNG was virtually defunct, and in August 2003 its three-year mandate expired. Another peace initiative, sponsored by the Intergovernmental Authority on Development (IGAD) in 2002 and 2003, initially appeared promising but quickly ran aground on familiar shoals – protracted disputes over representation in the talks, intransigence among Somali leaders over power-sharing, sabotage by spoilers, uninspired external mediation and active interference by Ethiopia and its Arab rivals Egypt and the Gulf states. The virtual proxy war which Ethiopia and the Arab states have played out in Somalia has been especially damaging. Arab states seek a strong central Somali state to counterbalance and outflank Ethiopia; Ethiopia seeks a weak, decentralised client state, and is willing to settle for ongoing state collapse rather than risk a revived Arab-backed government in Mogadishu. Both have provided military and financial support to their Somali clients, reinforcing the tendency towards violent political stalemate.

Until 11 September, Somalia's protracted anarchy posed a direct security threat mainly to the neighbouring states of Kenya and Ethiopia. Both countries have hosted hundreds of thousands of Somali refugees, and both have had to cope with the spillover of weapons flows, armed banditry and, in the case of Ethiopia, the use of Somalia as a base for insurgent groups. Since 1991, much of Kenya's north-east,which borders Somalia, has been a no-go area. The spillover of Somali lawlessness has even extended into the sprawling Nairobi slum of Eastleigh, a neighbourhood colonised by thousands of Somali refugees who are, rightly or wrongly, viewed by most Kenyans as a major source of armed crime in the city. Ethiopia has responded to the security threats posed by Somalia with military action, including support to Somali client groups along its border areas and direct incursions across the border. Kenya's response has been more muted, at times almost resembling a retreat away from the troubled border areas. However, following several al-Qaeda terrorist attacks inside Kenya in which Somalia was used as a transhipment point or safe haven by terrorists – the bombing of the US embassy in Nairobi in 1998, the bombing of a Mombasa hotel in 2002, and a foiled plan to attack the US embassy by light aircraft in June 2003 – Kenya has taken more assertive measures to contain the security threats posed by its neighbour's collapse.

Since the 11 September attacks, Somalia has attracted intense scrutiny in the war on terrorism, earning a permanent place on the shortlist of potential terrorist safe havens. The security threats posed by Somalia's collapsed state are now a matter of global significance. American and Western policy towards Somalia is now framed principally by counter-terrorism and security concerns, with an overriding emphasis on denying terrorist cells a base of operation in Somalia. Although Somalia has not to date proven to be an especially attractive base for al-Qaeda, its lawless environment could be exploited by terrorists. There is evidence that al-Qaeda operatives have used Somalia as a safe haven.

This paper analyses the dynamics of state collapse in Somalia, the interests which appear to perpetuate the Somalia crisis, the security threats which Somalia poses, and the challenges facing efforts to promote state-building and reconciliation. These issues are explored with the aim of shedding new light both on the Somali case, and on more general security concerns generated by collapsed states. Several specific questions frame the research:

- What is the nature of Somalia's protracted crisis, and what are the most significant trends over the past decade?
- Why has the Somalia crisis endured so long? To what extent is the crisis perpetuated by actors with political or economic interests in protracted state collapse?
- To what extent and in what ways is Somalia's ongoing state of collapse a security threat to the international community? How might terrorist groups seek to exploit it?
- What policies are most likely to meet the challenges of post-conflict reconstruction in Somalia? What are the most promising policy options for addressing global security concerns emanating from Somalia?

To answer the first two questions, the paper employs three analytic tools. First, it disaggregates the broad rubric of 'state collapse' in Somalia into three inter-related but distinct crises: (1) the protracted collapse of central government; (2) protracted armed conflict; and (3) lawlessness.[5] This taxonomy makes it much easier to identify and assess the interests of key actors, and may prove to be a valuable analytic device in other crises of state collapse. Certain actors may have a stake in perpetuating some of these crises, but not necessarily all three; this is an important observation if we are to comprehend some of the complex political manoeuvring by Somali elites.

Second, the paper seeks to track and explain significant changes in armed conflict, criminality and governance in Somalia over the past 13 years. Most writing on contemporary Somalia is relatively static in orientation. Warlordism, anarchy and armed conflict are taken as givens, presented as pathologies with little or no variation since 1991. A closer look, however, reveals a country undergoing dramatic change, driven in part by changing interests among the country's economic élites. Far from sinking into complete anarchy, Somalia has seen the rise of sub-state polities, some of which have assumed a fragile but nonetheless impressive capacity to provide core functions of government. Warfare has also undergone a transformation, with fighting becoming increasingly localised and intra-clan in nature. Finally, although the country remains vulnerable to lawless behaviour, the nature of criminality has changed dramatically. Looting and banditry still occur but are no longer endemic, as paid militia working for businessmen now protect most of the country's wealth. To safeguard their own commercial interests, these businessmen have financed efforts to control street violence, theft and banditry. Yet many of these same business elites are complicit in more pervasive 'white-collar' crime involving the manipulation of currency values, the import of counterfeit currency, the embezzlement of foreign aid, and other activities which would be considered illegal were a central government in place.

Third, the analysis draws on political economy of war theories to explore the proposition that the prolonged crisis in Somalia is not simply a product of diplomatic incompetence, missed opportunities and external conspiracy, but also an outcome which has been actively promoted by political and economic interest groups within Somalia. The claim that protracted state collapse and armed conflict are actually the desired outcome for key constituencies – an opportunity from which to profiteer, not a crisis to be solved – is one of the basic tenets of the literature on 'new wars' which is generating a growing body of research on complex political emergencies in Africa and elsewhere.[6] As this paper demonstrates, the analytic tools emerging from this approach are of considerable value in shedding light on aspects of the Somali crisis. The paper finds that powerful constituencies in Somalia profit from, and seek to promote, certain levels of conflict and certain types of lawlessness. Given Somalia's political situation, relatively small numbers of these spoilers form the equivalent of a 'veto coalition' over initiatives to control criminality and prevent armed clashes.

At the same time, the enduring nature of Somalia's collapsed central government is not so easily explained as an outcome which serves the parochial interests of some of its political and economic elite. On the contrary, we would expect the elite to reach a bargain in order to establish a 'paper state' (along the lines of Charles Taylor's government in Liberia from 1997 to 2003) – one which would attract foreign aid, embassies and the other lucrative trappings of sovereignty, but which would not become functional enough to threaten the illicit activities from which the elite profiteers. The fact that such a bargain has not been reached is a puzzle. The paper considers the extent to which risk-aversion and risk-management behaviour helps to explain this otherwise counter-intuitive outcome. It argues that zones of protracted state collapse tend to produce risk-averse decision-making by political and economic actors, which results in sub-optimal outcomes (such as the continued absence of a central government) and missed opportunities.[7]

The trend and interest analysis developed in the first half of the paper forms the basis for the next part, a threat assessment which considers potential security concerns emanating from Somalia. The conventional wisdom which emerged in the aftermath of the 9/11 attacks holds that collapsed states such as Somalia are in immediate danger as likely safe havens for terrorist groups seeking to operate beyond the rule of law. This paper argues that the conventional wisdom is a partial misreading, as evidence from Somalia and the Horn of Africa bears out. Terrorist networks are finding zones of state collapse to be useful, but not as originally expected. As safe havens, environments of complete state collapse such as Somalia are not ideal. The anarchy and insecurity of collapsed states makes terrorist cells vulnerable to extortion and betrayal; the paucity of Western targets makes them uninteresting; and the dearth of foreigners in these areas exposes foreign terrorists, reducing their ability to go unnoticed. In Somalia in particular, where foreign visitors are the subject of intense local scrutiny and discussion, secrecy is difficult to maintain over long periods. Terrorists, like mafias, prefer weak and corrupt government rather than no government at all. In the Horn of Africa, weak states such as Kenya and Tanzania are much more likely bases of operations for al-Qaeda. They feature sprawling, multi-ethnic urban areas where foreign operatives can go unremarked; corrupt law-enforcement agencies which can be bought off; and a rich array of Western targets.

Instead, a collapsed state such as Somalia is more likely to serve a niche role as a transit zone, through which men, money or materiel are quickly moved into the country and then across the borders of neighbouring states. Most evidence of terrorist activity in Somalia since 1997 points to exactly this kind of short-term operation. That is not to say that Somalia is not or cannot be used as a safe haven by individual terrorists – indeed, a few foreign terrorists have succeeded in maintaining a presence inside Somalia for an extended period. But for now at least, the number of suspected terrorists inside Somalia is small in comparison to most other states in the Horn of Africa and the Middle East.

The final portion of the paper considers the policy implications of this analysis for state-building, national reconciliation, post-conflict reconstruction and counter-terrorism. It argues that conventional diplomatic and post-conflict assistance is founded on a misdiagnosis which may actually yield counter-productive results. Misreadings of crises such as those in Somalia, Afghanistan and Liberia can result in mediation efforts which exacerbate and reignite conflicts; counter-terrorism measures which fail to advance the security of either the local population or the West; and post-conflict assistance which produces the very environment in which criminal and terrorist elements thrive – namely, a 'paper state' which enjoys the trapping of sovereignty, but without the capacity to control illicit activities within its borders.

Chapter 1

Reassessing Protracted State Collapse in Somalia

International diplomacy in Somalia has assumed a predictable pattern. Every couple of years, an external actor sets out to broker talks aimed at bringing national reconciliation and a government of national unity to the country. An initiative follows, leading to a peace conference attended by hundreds of eminent Somali political figures, usually in a fine hotel in a regional capital. The initiative invariably sparks fanfare and optimism, and sometimes considerable intolerance towards critics who raise doubts or concerns. Then familiar problems arise, involving disputes over representation, agendas or the composition of technical committees. The debate over who has the right to represent whom confounds the external mediators, who may be accustomed to a less chaotic political environment. Regional authorities, factional chairmen, militia commanders, self-proclaimed presidents, clan elders, religious figures, intellectuals and civil-society leaders all demand a place at the table, and disparage one another as illegitimate or irrelevant. Somali delegates devote almost all of their energies, not to discussing the critical issues dividing them, but rather to extended and unseemly haggling over the apportioning of positions in a future national government. Defections occur as individuals and groups fail to get what they feel they deserve. Increasingly frantic international mediators try to cajole the defectors, then brand them as spoilers. Delegates who remain sign accords which are never implemented, and then return home, often to a third country where they have resident status. The host country for the peace conference is left with a large unpaid bill. And as it becomes clear that yet another Somali peace process has failed, bitter blame ensues. Disillusionment sets in, and the appetite for Somali reconciliation is temporarily soured.

This cycle has yielded over a dozen failed national reconciliation processes since 1991. These repeated frustrations pose both a puzzle and a problem. How is it possible that Somalia can remain so resistant to efforts to revive its central government? How do we explain the protracted nature of this extraordinary case of state collapse?

For years, observers have relied on a standard set of explanations: that external diplomacy has been consistently misinformed and incompetent in its mediation efforts; that Somali leaders have been irresponsible and myopic in their quest for power and their stubborn refusal to compromise; that external states such as Ethiopia conspire to perpetuate state collapse and warfare in Somalia for their own reasons; that collective fear of the re-emergence of a predatory state undermines public support for peace-building processes; and that the powerful centrifugal force of Somali clannism works against coalitions and central authority, making quests to rebuild a Western-style central state a fool's errand. All of these theories have merit. But none fully captures the scope and dynamic of the Somali impasse, and all, to varying degrees, tend to be captive to residual thinking about the nature of conflict and the state in Somalia.

One part of the trouble encountered by analyses of Somalia is the tendency to group the country's multiple crises into a single syndrome. This shorthand has had the unwanted effect of disguising what are in fact a number of distinct crises, which exist independently of one another, have different dynamics requiring different remedies and pose different types of threats. Three distinct crises – state collapse, armed conflict and lawlessness – must be disaggregated if they are to be better understood and diagnosed.

The collapse of central government

The most dramatic and unique aspect of the Somali crisis has been the complete and protracted collapse of the central government. There has been no functional, central governing authority in Somalia since January 1991; efforts to re-establish a central state have been both numerous and unsuccessful. The most promising attempt was the Transitional National Government (TNG) announced in August 2000. Unfortunately, it failed to become minimally operational, was plagued by internal schisms, did not gain widespread bilateral recognition, and by 2002 appeared increasingly irrelevant. It formally expired in August 2003, the point at which its three-year mandate ended, though TNG President Abdiqassim Hassan Salad declared an extension. Even at the regional, district and municipal levels, formal administrations that have periodically popped up throughout the country have tended to have relatively short lives. The sole exception is the secessionist (and to date unrecognised) state of Somaliland in the north-western corner of the country, where a functioning central government has since 1996 provided modest levels of administration: keeping the peace, surviving a constitutional succession upon the death of the president and holding local and national elections.

The terms 'failed state' and 'collapsed state' have become throw-away lines to describe a wide range of crises.[1] In general, the terms describe a situation in which a central government has either lost control over a significant area of the country (territorial collapse), or has lost the ability or interest to exercise meaningful control over territory in which it has a physical presence (collapse of governing capacity) – or both. By this set of criteria, dozens of countries, especially in sub-Saharan Africa, qualify as failed states.[2] But in almost every other instance of state collapse, a weak, nominal central government has managed to maintain juridical sovereignty as a 'quasi-state', deemed to exist primarily because other states say it does.[3] Somalia's inability to retain even the most minimal central administration over the course of 13 years places the country in a class apart. Somalia is a failure among failed states.

The complete and sustained collapse of the central government in Somalia has created or contributed to numerous problems. But it is not *inherently* linked to other crises in Somalia, such as criminality and armed conflict. Indeed, Somalia has repeatedly shown that, in some places and at some times, communities, towns and regions can enjoy relatively high levels of peace, reconciliation, security and lawfulness despite the absence of a central authority. Moreover, a correlation between the existence of a functioning state authority and a state of peace and lawfulness is not borne out in the broader region. Somalis frequently and correctly point out that both criminality and deadly armed conflict are generally worse on the Kenyan side of the border, despite the existence of a sovereign state authority there. Those tempted to use Somaliland's impressive success as evidence to challenge this proposition may be baffled to encounter the popular opinion in the northwest that Somaliland enjoys peace, reconciliation, lawfulness and relative prosperity *despite*, not because of, the existence of a central government. The Somaliland administration is viewed not so much as a purveyor of law and stability as a relatively benign parasite created by a social contract brokered and enforced by clan elders and civil society. This is not to argue that a central state is unnecessary, or that the collapse of the state has not come at a very high cost to Somalis. It is only to assert that one cannot attribute all of Somalia's multiple woes to the collapse of the central government. One corollary to this observation is that strategies which presume that a revived central government is the solution to crime and armed conflict are incomplete and likely to result in disappointment.

In fact, a case can be made that attempts to revive a central state structure have actually exacerbated armed conflicts. State-building and peace-building are, in this view, two separate and in some respects mutually antagonistic enterprises. This is because the revival of a state structure is viewed in Somali quarters as a zero-sum game, creating winners and losers in a process with potentially very high stakes.[4] Clans and factions which gain control over a central government will use it to accrue economic resources at the expense of others, and to wield the law, patronage politics and a monopoly on the legitimate use of violence to dominate the rest. This is the only experience of the central state Somalis have ever known, and it tends to produce conflict rather than compromise whenever an effort is made to negotiate the establishment of a national government. It is not the *existence* of a functioning and effective central government which produces conflict, but rather the *process* of state-building which appears consistently to exacerbate instability and armed conflict.

This has generally held true for over a decade, from 1991 (when the Djibouti peace accord sparked the highly destructive war in Mogadishu between the militias of General Mohamed Farah Aideed and Ali Madhi) to the 2002 Kenyan-mediated peace process sponsored by IGAD. In 2002, political jockeying in anticipation of the IGAD talks was partly responsible for a spate of armed clashes that rendered south-central Somalia more insecure and inaccessible than at any time in the previous ten years.[5] As is common in collapsed states, a key flashpoint issue is over representation – the choices made by external mediators or technical committees over who may sit at the table. A seat at the negotiating table is viewed as an essential entrée for securing a position of power in a future government, so aspiring Somali political figures and their constituencies are simply unwilling to accept any formula which minimises or eliminates their presence. Decisions on the criteria for participation are thus viewed as more important than the peace negotiations themselves. Whatever choice of representation is made creates winners and losers, with the winners engaging in what one report describes as an 'unimaginative cake-cutting exercise in power-sharing by an unelected political elite'. Meanwhile, the losers plot to assume the role of spoiler.[6]

These debates over representation invariably produce conflict. When peace talks opt for factional leadership as the criteria for participation, what ensues is either deadly internal squabbles over chairmanship of the faction or the rapid fissuring of political organisations as aspiring delegates seek to establish their own faction. In Somalia, six factions populated the political landscape in early 1991. By 1995, there were about two dozen – all because factions were chosen by the UN as the basis of representation in Somali peace talks.[7] Alternatively, when peace talks focus on other criteria – such as administrative control of territory – conflicts break out over key towns or administrations. The Kenyan mediators of the 2002–2003 Eldoret peace talks wavered for some time over the question of criteria for participation, leading to armed conflicts over *both* factional chairmanship and control of regional administrations.[8] This goes some way towards explaining the serious armed clashes in 2002 in Puntland and Bay region, two areas which had until that time enjoyed prolonged peace and stability. In both cases, long-running leadership and clan tensions existed, but had been held in check – until the peace process was announced. The armed conflicts which subsequently erupted were at root efforts by rival political leaders to assert primacy over territory and leadership positions in order to ensure a place at the table in Eldoret.

The fact that efforts at state-building and national reconciliation have failed so consistently for more than a decade has made it easy for observers to conclude that politics and governance in Somalia is mired in anarchy. But a closer look reveals an impressive if fragile level of local governance. Collectively, these developments do not add up to anything resembling a conventional state. But the mosaic of local polities and informal social pacts which has evolved does provide Somali citizens with some level of 'governance', if not 'government'. In some cases, these informal and sub-national polities deliver more effective public order than in most neighbouring states in the Horn of Africa. The most visible manifestations of sub-national governance in Somalia are the formal, self-declared administrations. There are four levels of such polities: trans-regional, regional, district and municipal. Only one – the secessionist state of Somaliland, with an estimated population of two million[9] – has endured for more than a few years, but some of the others have still shown resilience and public support.

A number of regional and trans-regional authorities have come into existence in the past seven years, following the termination in March 1993 of the UNOSOM mission. Somaliland and Puntland (a non-secessionist, autonomous state in the arid north-east corner of the country, with a population of probably 600,000 people) are the only two such entities which have achieved much functional capacity, but a number of others – the Rahanweyn Resistance Army (RRA)'s administration of Bay and Bakool regions in 1998–2002 and the Benadir Regional Authority in 1996 – showed some initial promise. Strictly speaking, most of these regional and trans-regional polities are or were essentially clan homelands, reflecting a Somali impulse to pursue a 'Balkan solution' – or, more appropriate to the Somali context, 'clanustans'. Puntland's borders, for instance, are explicitly drawn along clan lines, encompassing the territory of the Harti in the northeast, including the portions of Sool and Sanaag regions which are contested by Somaliland and Puntland.[10] Even authorities which appear to be based on a pre-war regional unit are often thinly disguised clan polities. The periodic proclamation of a 'Hiranland', for instance, is really an attempt by the Hawadle clan to declare and control its own autonomous political unit, even though its remit extends only to the east bank of Hiran region.[11]

The fate of trans-regional and regional states in Somalia has been inversely related to the status of efforts to rebuild a national government. Trans-regional states were at their high-point in 1999, when both Somaliland and Puntland were operational and a nascent Rahanweyn administration in Bay and Bakool looked promising. The 'building-block' approach to Somali state-building, a policy favoured by external donors at the time, actively promoted these incipient states.[12] Once the Djibouti-led Arta peace process began to promote a national government in 2000, however, the regional states declined in importance. Now, with the demise of the TNG, variations on the building-block approach are regaining favour. External actors are placing great emphasis on political decentralisation as a point of departure for a resuscitated central state, a presumption which by definition revives the importance of regions and regional administrations. Somalis themselves remain deeply divided between 'unitarian' and 'federalist' camps, a split which was not easily papered over in the 2002–03 IGAD-sponsored talks in Kenya. Those advocating some form of decentralised, federal or even confederal system claim that it alone can guarantee protection for local communities (i.e. clans) from a central state dominated by another lineage. Unitarians fear that decentralisation will balkanise Somalia, destroying any hope of reviving Somali nationalism and providing neighbouring states with ample opportunity to divide and rule.[13] Among Somalis, preference for either the decentralised or unitarian vision of a future Somali state tends to be closely linked to the perceived advantages the options afford their lineage. Clans such as the Rahanweyn, which are relatively weak politically but which claim as their home territory some of the most valuable riverine and agricultural land in the country, are strong proponents of a federal solution. They view 'self-rule' as their only protection against larger, predatory clans, and expect federal states to possess the power to determine exclusionary citizenship in order to pre-empt colonisation by land-hungry Somalis from other clans. Conversely, some lineages, especially the Hawiye clan-family, now dominate the political and economic life of Mogadishu, and hence view federalism as a thinly-veiled attempt to rob them of their 'turn' to enjoy the fruits of a central state.

Despite these differences, one significant trend in political discussions of a future Somali state is a much broader agreement that some sort of decentralised and federal system is probably inevitable. The details of such a political system are now the focal point of disagreement, with proponents of a more centralised state advocating federal models which minimise the authority and financial autonomy of regional units. Sharp disagreement also exists over the administrative units of decentralisation, with some insisting on the use of pre-war regional boundaries, while others, such as Puntland leader Abdullahi Yusuf, argue for recognition of autonomous trans-regional states. The fact that some variation of a federal system is increasingly viewed as inevitable will set in motion renewed efforts to form or consolidate regional states in coming years – almost certainly in Puntland, Bay and Bakool regions and the Middle Shabelle, and possibly in Hiran, Gedo and the Kismayo area. If these regional states are formed as 'clanustans', they will trigger conflict and at worst ethnic cleansing. In southern Somalia, decades of migration and settlement mean that much of the ethnic topography resembles the patch-quilt of a Bosnia rather than the ethno-state of a Puntland; here, the building-block approach is only viable if regional polities are ethnically heterogeneous experiments in co-existence and power-sharing, rather than tools of ethnic hegemony.

The past 12 years have, however, produced ample evidence throughout Somalia that localised politics is not necessarily more benign to minorities.[14] Instead, regional and local administrations have tended to be tools of domination wielded by the larger or more powerful clans against weaker groups. The dominant clan typically insists on control over formal political structures; monopolises employment and contracts with aid agencies; restricts commercial competition from weaker clans; and at worst engages in forced labour and land-grabbing at the expense of minority lineages. Some regions are better than others, but nowhere are weaker lineages accorded a 'fair share' of political and economic resources. Somaliland is without question the most promising regional polity. There, the powerful Isaaq clan dominates both commercial and political activity, but has taken a relatively enlightened approach to smaller clans, in large part out of political necessity – the Somaliland secessionist bid, in which the Isaaq are major stakeholders, is contingent on the perceived legitimacy of the state, which would be badly damaged were non-Isaaq clans to boycott the experiment. This approach was put to the test in May 2002 when the president of Somaliland, Mohamed Farah Egal (himself an Isaaq) passed away, leaving the presidency to Vice-President Dahir Riyale Kahin, a member of the Gadabursi clan. The Isaaq political leadership accepted the succession to a non-Isaaq, a move which enhanced the political legitimacy of Somaliland considerably in the eyes of a still-cautious international community.

In the south of Somalia, local polities have tended to be much less generous to smaller and weaker clans; indeed, most local and regional polities in south-central Somalia are associated with clannish hegemony dressed up as formal administration. In Gedo region in the south-west corner of the country, the Marehan clan monopolises political and economic life at the expense of the Rahanweyn and others; weaker clans not only go under-represented in the various administrations which periodically pop up, but are in places deprived of farmland, pasture and wells. The Marehan have used their privileged political position (in the 1970s and 1980s as the clan of President Siyad Barre, and in the 1990s as the strongest militia in the region) to colonise new land and settlements at the expense of neighbouring clans in the region. The Rahanweyn in turn declare non-members to be 'outsiders' in Bay region, even though a sizeable population of non-Rahanweyn Somalis lived and worked in Bay region prior to the war. In Hiran region, the Hawadle clan, which dominates the east bank, has apportioned some economic opportunities to weaker rival clans on the west bank, but has prevented Haber Gedir clansmen from returning to the regional capital to reclaim their homes and businesses. Along parts of the Jubba and Shabelle rivers, militarily strong clans – in some cases newcomers who occupy territory by force – not only assume complete control over towns, but have also been charged with forcibly conscripting local minorities and expropriating their farmland. The important port city of Kismayo has enjoyed relative peace and stability in recent years, but this has been imposed by two outside clans, the Marehan and Haber Gedir/Ayr, which have occupied the town under the banner of the 'Jubba Valley Alliance' in order to profit from import–export activities at the port, which they monopolise. In Middle Shabelle region, militia from the dominant Abgal clan have attempted to force minority farming communities there to declare themselves Abgal or risk attack. Clearly, the trend towards political decentralisation has the potential to degenerate into ethnic cleansing if it is not executed with considerable local sensitivity.[15]

The key variable in whether regional administrations are likely to yield co-existence and power-sharing, rather than ethnic hegemony, appears to depend on the primary purpose which the regional polities serve. If they come into existence solely as stepping stones designed to culminate in a central state, they are more likely to produce conflict and encourage ethnic domination at the local level, even as they fail to deliver basic services. This is for several reasons. First, when viewed as building-blocks of a central government,

Major Somali lineages

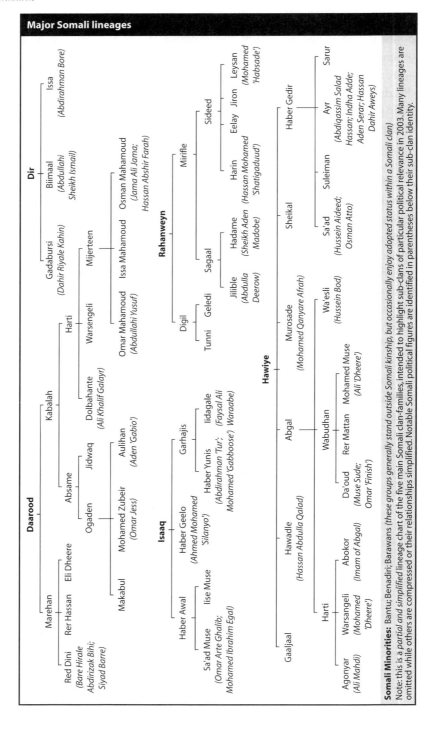

Somali Minorities: Bantu; Benadiri; Barawans (these groups generally stand outside Somali kinship, but occasionally enjoy adopted status within a Somali clan)

Note: this is a *partial and simplified lineage* chart of the five main Somali clan-families, intended to highlight sub-clans of particular political relevance in 2003. Many lineages are omitted while others are compressed or their relationships simplified. Notable Somali political figures are identified in parentheses below their sub-clan identity.

federal states attract political figures whose sole interest is in using them to secure a senior position in the national government. The regional states become the new means of securing a place in a central administration. This invites intense power struggles by individuals (and their constituents). These political figures have no interest in actually administering the federal state; their focus is on the capital. This 'seat-banking' behaviour has already occurred in Puntland, where Abdullahi Yusuf has presided (and fought) over control for the sole purpose of parlaying it into a top position in a future national government. The so-called governor of Hiran region has done much the same there; he has been actively hostile to efforts to build local administration in his region, biding his time for a ministerial position in Mogadishu.

Second, in the building-block scenario each federal state will be viewed locally as the 'seat' for a particular clan; there will be little tolerance for the competing claims of other clans resident in the region. Because there are invariably more clans than states, each will struggle to ensure control over a federal state. As with factions in the early 1990s, this will yield one of two results – either bloody battles for control, or a multiplication of new states to accommodate every lineage's demand for its 'own' home base. Since Somali clans are almost limitlessly fissile, this process could yield a continual multiplication of new federal units.

Regional polities which emerge independently of a cumulative state-building process stand a better chance of avoiding conflict. Reconciliation and local governance pursued for its own sake tends to reflect a broadly shared need in the local community for cooperative, predictable, lawful relations between clans, usually in order to promote commerce.

The political administrative unit which has received the least amount of external support but which has produced the most actual day-to-day governance in Somalia is at the municipal and (in Mogadishu) neighbourhood level. In the immediate post-UNOSOM period, this 'radical localisation' of politics tended to manifest itself mainly in informal, overlapping polities loosely held by clan elders and others.[16] Over the course of the second half of the 1990s, these local polities became more structured and institutionalised.[17] Different types of local polity have emerged in Somalia, but the most common manifestation has been a coalition of clan elders, intellectuals, businessmen and Muslim clergy, which oversees, finances and administers a sharia court. These coalitions are shaky, laced with tensions over power and resources. Relations between businessmen and clan elders can be especially testy, as the elders regularly seek funds from wealthier clansmen to cover costs ranging from blood-payment compensation to travel expenses. Intellectuals – anyone with a secondary-school education or university degree – chafe at what they view as the clannish and uneducated behaviour of the elders, sheikhs and merchants. The clan elders themselves can prove fickle about controlling young armed men from their own clan, and are sometimes complicit in the very acts of banditry which the sharia courts attempt to police. But when conditions are right, these groups are able to cobble together a modest judicial and law-enforcement structure.

Several features of these sharia courts stand out. First, they have been widely embraced and supported by local communities as a means of restoring the rule of law. Second, they have usually remained under the control of traditional, moderate elements – the clan elders, the businessmen and the sheikhs making up this system are usually staunchly opposed to radical Islam.[18] Third, these sharia court systems have remained local in nature, rarely able to project their authority beyond a town or district, and rarely able to exercise jurisdiction over clans which are not parties to the court administration. They thus offer rule of law within, but not between, clans, though they often facilitate inter-clan relations. Fourth, they have proved fragile and susceptible to spoilers. Where they have succeeded in curbing lawlessness, this has never been via direct confrontation with a powerful warlord. Instead, it has tended to occur in areas where the power of local warlords and militia is already on the wane for other reasons. Finally, the sharia courts appear to come and go in cycles, and are currently in what appears to be an early phase of ascendance following a decline in 1999–2001. Their current re-emergence in parts of southern Somalia is linked in part to the failure of the TNG and the related rise of insecurity, and is a reflection of local efforts to provide core functions of governance.[19]

In some locations – notably the towns of Borama, Hargeisa, Luuq, Jowhar, Beled Weyn and Merka – local polities constitute incipient municipalities which do more than simply keep the peace via a sharia court. They have also at times managed to provide some basic services, operating piped water systems, regulating marketplaces and collecting modest levels of taxes and user fees to cover salaries. Typically, these successful municipalities have been led by dedicated, professional mayors working closely with local non-governmental organisations (NGOs), clan elders and businesses. These successes usually involve partnership with UN agencies and international NGOs committed to local capacity-building, and which provide much of the funding for municipal projects. In some cases, innovative partnerships have resulted – the management of several UNICEF municipal piped water systems has been outsourced to a multi-clan consortium of businessmen, who have run the water system effectively and transparently as a money-making venture. As with the sharia courts, effective municipalities have enjoyed enormous popularity in the local community, but have also proved vulnerable to the machinations of warlords and jealous politicians, and to clan tensions. Most of the municipalities mentioned above have risen and fallen (and sometimes risen again) since the mid-1990s.

What has emerged in Somalia by way of 'governance' in the past decade has not so much resembled the 'jagged-glass pattern of city-states, shanty-states [and] nebulous and anarchic regionalisms' depicted in Robert Kaplan's famous 1994 portrait of failed states,[20] but rather a loose constellation of commercial city-states and villages separated by long stretches of pastoral statelessness. In the towns, the sharia courts and municipal authorities do what they can to impose the basic rule of law. Business partnerships create extensive commercial ties, which transcend clan and conflict. This imbues Somali society with a dense network of communication and cooperative relations that are often critical in managing conflict and taking the edge off what appears to be anarchy. The pastoral zones have never come under the effective control of a state, so the collapse of the state has not been as traumatic for nomadic populations as outsiders often presume. There, protection and access to resources have long been secured through a combination of blood payment groups (*diya*), customary law (*xeer*), negotiation (*shir*) and the threat of force. Over the past decade, clan elders in pastoral areas have partially restored their authority and devote most of their energies to managing relations with neighbouring clans. Where clan territory abuts an international border, elders have also assumed a role as diplomatic envoys to state authorities in Ethiopia or Kenya, working out cooperative relations on policing banditry, smuggling and the spillover of local disputes. Although some clan elders are uneducated and illiterate, they have nonetheless been quick to adapt new technology to their diplomatic work; VHF radios and mobile phones allow them to communicate across clan and conflict lines.

These extensive and intensive mechanisms for managing conflict and providing a modest level of security are virtually invisible to external observers, whose sole preoccupation is often with the one structure which actually provides the least amount of rule of law to Somalis – the central state. Indeed, whether the discussion is about the central state or sub-national administrations, an enormous gulf separates foreigners and Somalis in the consideration and conception of central government. For external actors, a responsive and effective state is an essential prerequisite for development – a proposition enshrined in virtually every World Bank and UN strategy. For Somalis, the state is an instrument of accumulation and domination, enriching and empowering those who control it and exploiting and harassing the rest. These different perceptions often result in external and national actors talking past one another in discussions about the rebuilding of the central government.

Protracted armed conflict

Somalia has seen intermittent armed conflict since 1988. Armed clashes were most destructive and widespread in 1988–92, when the country was in a genuine state of civil war. Since the UNOSOM intervention in 1993–95, clashes have been generally localised, brief and much less costly in terms of loss of life and damage to property. Some regions of the country – notably Puntland – were almost entirely spared war in the 1990s, while other locations have, since 1995, enjoyed relatively long stretches of, if not peace, then at least an absence of armed conflict. Conflict has thus not been synonymous with state collapse. Peace can and does exist despite the absence of a central state. Likewise, the establishment of a central government would not be likely to eliminate armed conflict. Instead, it would transform at least some of the conflicts into insurrections, guerrilla movements or secessionism, pitting government forces against rejectionists.

The trend of diminished armed conflict in Somalia was

temporarily reversed in 2002.[21] In that year, multiple and in some instances serious outbreaks of armed conflict from Gedo region to Puntland produced casualty levels which again qualified the country as a zone of civil war.[22] These conflicts were triggered by a number of factors, but some can be attributed to political manoeuvring linked to the IGAD-sponsored peace talks in October. Collectively, they plunged southern and central Somalia into greater levels of insecurity than at any time since 1995.

Not only has the severity of warfare in Somalia changed since 1991–92, but its nature has as well. In the early 1990s, armed conflicts were mainly inter-clan in nature, pitting large lineage groups against one another. Initially, this meant warfare between the most powerful clan-families in the south – the Darood versus the Hawiye. These wars were characterised by sweeping and fast-moving campaigns across much of southern Somalia, from the outskirts of Mogadishu to the Kenyan border. The warring militias of the Darood clan's Somali Patriotic Movement (SPM)[23] and the Hawiye clan's United Somali Congress (USC) often ceded or gained hundreds of square kilometres of territory in a day, in fighting waged mainly off the back of battlewagons known as 'technicals'. Both sides committed atrocities – massacres and rape – against civilians belonging to the wrong clan, or to a weak and defenceless clan. Pillaging and looting of captured territory were an essential aspect of warfare, providing war booty to otherwise unpaid militiamen and the financial backers of their clan's warlord.[24]

By late 1991, the centrifugal forces which have driven Somalia's fragmentation led to a new and highly destructive phase of warfare, in which both the Hawiye and Darood clan-families fell into deadly internal quarrels. In Mogadishu, the split between the Hawiye/Abgal (led by self-declared president Ali Madhi) and Hawiye/Haber Gedir clans (led by Madhi's rival General Hussein Farah Aideed, head of the Somali National Alliance (SNA)) erupted into serious conflict in November 1991. The extensive and often indiscriminate use of mortars and rocket-propelled grenades levelled much of central Mogadishu and caused thousands of casualties. Heavy fighting was waged to gain or hold single city blocks. To the south, tensions within the Darood culminated in clashes in and around Kismayo, pitting Ogadeni clan militias led by Colonel Omar Jess against the coalition of Marehan, Mijerteen and other clans in General Morgan's Somali Patriotic Movement (SPM).

One of the most significant trends of armed conflict since 1992 has been the devolution of warfare to lower and lower levels of clan lineages. With a few exceptions, most armed conflicts since 1995 have consisted of extended family feuds. Periodic clashes in Mogadishu are now almost always within the Abgal or Haber Gedir clans, not between them. Fighting in the Medina neighbourhood in 2001–2003 involved competing leaders and militias from within a single Abgal sub-clan (the Da'oud). Likewise, the Haber Gedir clan has long since ceased to be a cohesive political unit; splits between the Ayr, Sa'ad, Suleiman and other sub-clans animate most of the fighting and political intrigue within it. The Rahanweyn now fight among themselves in Baidoa, not against the Marehan and Haber Gedir; the fighting which plagues Gedo is an intramural squabble of the Marehan clan, and the Mijerteen have fought over control of Puntland.

This fragmentation and devolution of warfare to much lower levels has many implications. It has meant that conflict has become much more localised; clashes are contained within a sub-clan's territory or neighbourhoods. Conflicts are shorter and less deadly, in part because of limited support from lineage members for such internal squabbles, in part because clan elders are in a better position to intervene, and in part because money and ammunition is scarcer.[25] Conflicts are also less predictable, often precipitated by a theft or other misdemeanour. Atrocities against civilians are now almost unheard of, as combatants are much more likely to be held accountable in subsequent clan reconciliation processes. Pillaging and looting are less common, in part because little territory is gained or lost in localised clashes, and in part because commodities worth stealing are generally in the hands of businessmen with paid security forces to protect them. 'Warlords' have become less of a factor, as only a few have the funds to pay a militia, and even those which do find it harder to manipulate clannism given the increased (and renewed) linkages between clans for commercial purposes.[26] Since 1999, businessmen in Mogadishu who had previously provided funds to warlords in their clan have refused to pay, instead financing their own militias. Salaries are generally low – a dollar or two per day per militiaman. Nonetheless, with few exceptions gunmen fight for whoever will pay them, not for a clan or a cause – though in the event the clan is under attack, elders will mobilise gunmen temporarily. The paucity of opportunities to loot, and the low salaries offered to militiamen, means that the status and earning power of a gunman are not what they used to be, prompting a gradual, spontaneous demobilisation and reducing incentives for the new generation of young men to take up arms as a form of employment.

International efforts to negotiate an end to these armed conflicts are uncommon. Instead, reconciliation efforts are generally the domain of clan elders, with the international community simply suspending aid operations in battle zones until security is deemed adequate for staff to return. The main exception is the role Ethiopia has unsuccessfully attempted to play in mediating armed clashes between its clients. Otherwise, external mediation tends to focus on state-building, not peace-building, despite the fact that the average Somali needs – and benefits more immediately from – a state of peace than a revived central government.

Lawlessness and criminality

The third crisis facing Somalia is lawlessness and criminality. An enduring stereotype linked to Somalia's protracted state collapse is the 'Mad Max' anarchy of young, armed gunmen riding technicals and terrorising citizens. The collapse of the state has created conditions ripe for lawless behaviour, just as outbreaks of armed conflict also create an environment conducive to opportunistic crime. But Somalia has repeatedly shown that informal systems of governance can ensure the rule of law, and in some instances surprisingly high levels of personal security. In fact, one of Somalia's most intriguing paradoxes is how dramatically and quickly the rule of law and personal security can change. A town or neighbourhood which is notoriously bandit-ridden can within a year boast stalls of street-corner money-changers and open roads; likewise, towns lauded for their peace and security can fall quickly into lawlessness.

Where Somali communities have been able to establish and maintain a high level of lawful behaviour and personal security, this has almost always been accomplished either by clan customary law (*xeer*), the enforcement of blood payments (*diya*) for wrongs committed, or the application of Islamic law by local sharia courts. The latter complements rather than replaces traditional sources of law. Several necessary but not sufficient conditions must obtain for customary law to successfully maintain order. One is the restoration of the authority and responsibility of clan elders, who negotiate all disputes. A second is the establishment of a rough balance of power within local clan groupings. The capacity of a lineage to seek revenge for a wrong committed is critical in inducing other clans to seek the settlement of disputes through customary law. Weak and powerless clans (including minority or low-caste clans) rarely enjoy the protection of enforced customary law; the best such lineages can do is to seek client status with a more powerful clan and hope that it fulfils its obligations. Clans constantly look for a rough balance of power both to avoid being overrun, and to enhance routine patterns of cooperation, reinforced by repeated adherence to customary law by all sides – what international relations theorists would call 'regimes'.

Like armed conflict, lawlessness in Somalia has changed considerably over the course of the 1990s. The early years of civil war – from 1988 to 1992 – featured a level of impunity and gratuitous violence which has long since passed. Wholesale looting, rape and murder associated with armed clashes rarely occur. In instances where such atrocities do take place, as in intra-Rahanweyn conflicts in 2003 (when armed groups raped young women from rival sub-clans and engaged in ethnic cleansing around Baidoa), they provoke local and international condemnation.[27] Violent crimes and theft are much more likely to be addressed via customary law and blood payments than was the case before, serving both as a deterrent to would-be criminals, and as a reassurance to communities that criminals cannot commit crimes with complete impunity. Neighbourhoods and towns (often of mixed clan composition) have in some places organised the equivalent of 'neighbourhood-watch' systems, sometimes absorbing former gunmen into paid protection forces. Vigilante justice is not unknown against both individual criminals and gangs – often by their own kinsmen.[28] Militia gangs which terrorised villages in the early 1990s have increasingly 'settled down', making arrangements to 'tax' a portion of village harvests in return for protection. Such protection rackets and mafioso behaviour are hardly ideal, and sometimes engender local resistance, but they do nonetheless provide a more predictable security environment for local communities. In some cases, these arrangements have moved into a grey area between extortion and taxation, between protection racket and nascent security force.

The rule of law in Somalia was in the past never associated with a formal judiciary and police force. Most of the law and order

Somalia enjoyed prior to the late 1980s – and Somalia was unquestionably one of the safest places in Africa – was a reflection of a social contract more than the capacity of the police. Most Somalis took their legal disputes to a local sheikh or elder for mediation or adjudication, rather than to a court of law. The extensive and costly capacity-building efforts of international aid agencies to support the police and judiciary throughout Somalia often presume that they are rebuilding a set of institutions, when actually they are trying to make them functional for the first time.

Lawless behaviour remains a serious problem, especially in the more troubled south. Ironically, the most egregious crimes (if measured in value stolen or lives lost) are committed by many of the country's top political and business leaders, whom the international community convenes for peace conferences. This includes inciting communal violence for political purposes, the embezzlement of foreign aid funds, the introduction of counterfeit currency (which, by creating hyperinflation, robs average Somalis of most of their savings), huge land grabs, the export of charcoal (illegal under the past government and highly destructive environmentally), and involvement in piracy. This criminal behaviour tends to get less attention than street crimes such as carjacking, murder and kidnapping, which are usually perpetrated by gangs or individuals. These crimes are at epidemic proportions in some places, but pale in comparison to the cost of 'white-collar crime' by the political and business leadership.

Kidnapping is an increasingly troubling problem, both for international agencies and local Somalis. It is most common in Mogadishu, but not unheard-of elsewhere. Kidnapping falls into several different categories. The most common is kidnapping for profit, which has become a major criminal activity because it is currently one of the few profitable ventures for Mogadishu street criminals, even though ransoms are often small (as low as a few hundred dollars). This tends to target Somalis linked to a likely source of funds, such as a job with an international agency or family members in the diaspora. UN agencies have been plagued by kidnaps of national staff. Somalis from weak or minority clans are especially vulnerable. Some armed gangs have come to specialise in kidnapping. There is evidence that these gangs pass on kidnap victims to a more powerful warlord for a fee, at which point the warlord assumes the risk of negotiating for a ransom. Clan elders who mediate the release of the kidnap victim also routinely receive a portion of the ransom for their services, giving them a stake in the industry.[29]

A second type of kidnapping involves debtors who have defaulted on or repeatedly postponed repayments. Somalis lend and borrow an extraordinary amount of money to one another, as part of the extensive web of mutual obligations that are at the heart of lineage-based societies. Not surprisingly, rates of defaulting are also quite high. Kidnapping in these cases involves the ultimate collateral – the debtor themselves – whose family must scrape together the funds to secure their release. Some high-visibility kidnappings, including of members of parliament and ministers in the TNG, have been debt-collection actions.

Third, kidnapping is in some instances a political tool, designed to frighten off international agencies or humiliate a political opponent by demonstrating his incapacity to control an area he claims to administer. The dramatic kidnapping of UN and international NGO staff members in north Mogadishu in March 2001 was explicitly intended to humiliate the TNG and expose its inability to provide international aid workers with security, in order to scuttle a proposed UN peace-building presence in Mogadishu. Militias have also targeted wealthy businessmen from their own clan in order to finance armed attacks, now that businesses are less willing to fund militias themselves. Whatever the motive, internationals travelling and working in parts of southern Somalia are now at considerable risk of kidnap; this is one of the main reasons why aid agencies have cut back so substantially on the number of international staff members in the field.

Somalia's state of lawlessness has not attracted the level of transnational crime one might expect. In theory, the protracted collapse of formal law-enforcement capacity should provide an attractive safe haven for a wide range of criminal elements – terrorists, smugglers (of drugs, guns, people and other contraband), money-launderers, pirates and criminals on the run. In fact, Somalia has proven to be relatively inhospitable terrain for international criminals. Foreign criminals are at the mercy of the same sources of insecurity as those which plague international aid workers – they are prone to extortion, threats and betrayal from Somali hosts seeking to profit from their presence, and their activities and whereabouts are poorly kept secrets among Somalis, who are extremely alert to the presence of foreigners. Somalia is a reminder that mafias and other organised crime flourish not where the rule of law is absent, but rather where it is corruptible. Nonetheless, the misuse of Somalia's lawless environment by external criminals and terrorists should remain an item of enduring concern. As discussed in chapter 3, the greatest terrorist threat posed by Somalia's collapsed state will almost certainly be its use, not as a fixed operational base, but as a short-term point of transit for men, money and materiel into other states in the Horn of Africa, and perhaps as a site for safe houses where terrorists can assume new identities or simply disappear.[30]

Chapter 2

Interests and Risk in a Collapsed State

Explanations of Somalia's protracted crises ask two distinct but not entirely antithetical questions: are the crises enduring *despite* the fact that key Somali constituencies would benefit from peace and political stability; or are they enduring *because* key interests are served by prolonging a state of collapse, war and lawlessness? Most diplomatic initiatives have presumed the former, leading logically to certain prescriptive actions ranging from civil society peace-building workshops to national reconciliation conferences – all designed to promote greater understanding and communication. The latter proposition – that the protracted Somali crisis actually reflects the interests and objectives of key actors – suggests that there is a method to the madness, that the crisis is driven by a certain level of rationality, expressed in the pursuit of well-defined individual or group interests. How feasible is it to conclude that Somalia's triple crises of state collapse, armed conflict and lawlessness have endured because that is the outcome which key players seek?

When one considers the evidence of the past decade in the light of the political economy of war theory, several things become clear. First, an impressive but shrinking set of actors have interests that are served by protracted conflict and lawlessness, and who appear actively and successfully to promote both. But there are few Somali players who clearly benefit from complete state collapse. The 'war economy' theory is thus of use in explaining part, but not all, of the Somali debacle. Second, the interests of some social and economic groups have changed considerably over time, prompting in some instances marked changes in attitude towards state- and peace-building projects. This malleability of interests may constitute one of the most important opportunities for external actors seeking to promote peace and the rule of law. To the extent that interests, not identity, are increasingly at the root of Somalia's crises, and to the extent that the interests of key players can be shaped or reshaped, external actors may be able to better promote peace-building in Somalia.[1]

One useful aspect of this approach is that it forces us to conduct an inventory of actors in Somalia, organised not only around the question 'whose interests are served by conflict, state collapse and/or lawlessness?', but also around the question 'whose interests matter?'. This highlights the central issue of power, or – more precisely – veto power.

There has in fact been a substantial shift in the fortunes of different political actors in Somalia since 1991. Factions have virtually disappeared from the political landscape, a remarkable fact considering that they were the centrepiece of reconciliation efforts for over six years in the early to mid-1990s. Warlords and militia leaders are with few exceptions much less powerful than they were in the early years of the crisis. Conversely, businessmen have emerged as a major political force in urban centres, and now operate with considerable autonomy. Clan elders have also gradually reasserted some of their authority, and civil society leaders play a more robust (though still modest) role. In addition, Islamic social movements such as al-Islah have come to assume a prominent role as providers of health care and education in Mogadishu, and constitute one of the most organised networks in contemporary Somalia.

Despite these changes, one fact has remained relatively constant – namely that there exists a wide range of players who are not necessarily powerful enough to shape a peace accord or a government, but who nonetheless enjoy a veto over political developments that they do not like. It takes relatively little to scuttle peace talks or render an administration stillborn. Local and regional initiatives, promised to seal a peace between warring clans or operate a local sharia court administration, have frequently been torpedoed by a small gang of gunmen, a single warlord or a group of clan elders corrupted by small bribes. Thus, one answer to the question 'whose interests matter?' is that a broad section of Somali society possesses veto power over state-building, peace-building and law enforcement. This makes negotiating towards those objectives all the more difficult, and means that mediators need to take great care to ensure that proposed power-sharing and resource-sharing formulas are acceptable to a wide range of actors, some of whom may not have enough political legitimacy or influence to attend a peace conference, but who nonetheless retain enough power to sabotage the results. When one adds the numerous external actors who possess the interests and capacity to spoil unwelcome political developments (Ethiopia is the most obvious but not sole example), brokering an accord becomes an even more challenging task.

Spoilers in Somalia come in three types. One type comprises actors who seek to undermine efforts at state-building or peace-building because they are dissatisfied with what they have been accorded. These 'situational' spoilers can be individuals or whole clans. In some instances they may have legitimate grievances, though in most cases their motive is greed. In theory, they can be bought into a state-building venture with appropriate concessions. At the 2002–03 peace talks in Kenya, a crucial swing-group in the talks were a loose group of militia leaders, mainly from the Mogadishu area, known as the Group of Eight; their positions and actions at the talks – namely threatening to walk away from them – closely reflected a desire to leverage better positions in the proposed transitional government. Another group did in fact walk away in September 2003, forming a new coalition, the National Salvation Council (NSC).[2]

A second type are 'intrinsic' spoilers. These have a fundamental interest in maintaining a state of lawlessness, state collapse and/or armed conflict. War criminals are the most obvious candidates, but a host of other social and economic groups can also fall into this category: young gunmen, merchants of war, individuals and groups holding valuable state and private assets which they would be likely to lose were government and peace re-established. Whole clans have benefited from armed occupation and the settlement of towns and valuable riverine land in southern Somalia over the course of the war, and will be unlikely to accept accords which require relinquishing these spoils.[3] They will only accept a 'victor's peace', which gives them both political power and an unchallenged right to occupy the lands won in wartime. It is this set of interests that 'new war' theories are best suited to explain.

A final and more complex set of spoilers are those who could potentially benefit from peace, governance and the rule of law, but who choose to scuttle initiatives that might alter an operating environment which, while not ideal, is at least familiar and in which they have learned to profit. Some of the major businessmen in Mogadishu believed to have quietly subverted the TNG fall into this category. A revived government could presumably generate very profitable opportunities, by way of property rental to foreign embassies and aid agencies and contracts for post-war construction projects. But the risk involved in a revived state exercising its prerogative to regulate, tax or even nationalise a business enterprise appears too great.

Interests in protracted conflict

The interest groups which have benefited from and promoted armed conflicts in Somalia have changed considerably over time. In the early years of the crisis (1990–92), an overwhelming array of interests profiteered from armed conflict and the humanitarian crisis it provoked. Warlords used the threat of armed clashes to maintain support, sought conflicts and conquest to provide war booty for their militiamen and provoked famine to attract relief agencies and food aid, which became a major source of revenue. Militiamen fed their families by pillaging occupied villages and government buildings. Some profiteered from the diversion of food aid, the export of scrap metal and gun sales. Entire clans acquired, by armed conquest and occupation, valuable territory in Mogadishu and riverine regions. Many of the features of protracted conflict depicted in the political economy of war literature closely match patterns of conflict in southern Somalia in the early 1990s, except for the fact that Somalia's war economy has at no point attracted the level of external economic interest seen in mineral- or timber-rich countries such as Sierra Leone, Angola and Congo.

In the post-UNOSOM period, however, the constituencies which benefit from war have shrunk. The fact that warfare in Somalia has gradually diminished in scope suggests a possible causal link between interests and conflict. Warlords have seen their capacity to foment conflict reduced – though not eliminated – due to a loss of financial support from businessmen and from their own war-weary clans. Opportunities for looting following armed conflict are much more limited, reducing incentives for militiamen to fight. Most businessmen who initially profited from a war economy have moved into quasi-legitimate commerce in imports–exports, telecommunications and transport, and in some cases hold valuable fixed assets which cannot be relocated in times of war. They thus have a greater interest in peace and paying customers, rather than armed clashes and famine victims. Some still indulge in questionable or illegal business activities, but these do not require, and are not well served by, armed conflict. War is now, for the most part, bad for business. The net result of these changed interests is that the armed conflicts which exist today in Somalia tend to be driven less by economic interests (as they were in 1991–92) and more by the parochial political agendas of individual leaders. Brief outbreaks of conflict, triggered by feuds between militias and clans over such matters as carjackings, murders, land and contract disputes and taxes at roadblocks, are generally contained quickly by clan elders.

In sum, the interests perpetuating armed conflict in Somalia are far less potent and extensive than in earlier phases of the crisis, and those interests in favour of peace – or at least a suspension of armed conflict – have grown appreciably. Warfare is no longer an 'instrument of enterprise' as it was in the early years of the crisis. Although Somalia experienced a resurgence of more widespread insecurity and armed clashes in 2002, these were for the most part parochial, politically driven clashes serving the interests of an increasingly small group.

But while constituencies promoting actual armed conflict may be smaller and less powerful than in the past, there remain political and economic interests which successfully promote political tensions and communal distrust. Here, the distinction between armed conflict and an absence of reconciliation is important. In many places in Somalia, warfare has been replaced by tense stand-offs and divided communities – neither war nor peace. Most towns exist in such a condition, divided sometimes by a relatively hard 'green line' and in other cases by neighbourhood enclaves. Riverine towns are frequently split along clan lines by the river itself. Mogadishu is a patchwork of clan strongholds (though no neighbourhoods in the capital are exclusively single-clan, and some are relatively mixed). In the northeast, Galkayo is sharply split between Mijerteen in the north of the town and Haber Gedir in the south; the northern portion is part of the state of Puntland, but the south is not. Beled Weyn town is divided between the Hawadle clan and the Gaaljaal and other smaller clans. Some of these enclaves are simply a legacy of clannish settlement patterns from pre-war times; others are divisions which have been hardened or even created by the civil war. Whatever their origin, these 'green lines' and the absence of reconciliation which they represent have taken on a life of their own, as political and economic interests have assumed a stake in their existence.

Politically, a 'cold peace' in a divided city or district is vital for militia leaders whose value to their clan rests mainly on their ability to protect it against attack by other clan militias. Where the threat of attack is reduced – by a peace accord and normalised relations, for instance – militia leaders are marginalised, and civilian political leaders challenge their authority. With few exceptions, militia leaders in Somalia are not widely popular within their own clan constituencies. In some cases, they are viewed as a nuisance, as unwanted warlords, and are held responsible for the misery their wars have caused. But in times of political crisis, tension and threat, these militia leaders are needed by their people, and enjoy their support as protectors against the external threat. Not surprisingly, such warlords do all they can to stir up communal distrust and tensions. They sabotage reconciliation efforts by staging brief armed incidents, orchestrate a crime such as a carjacking or looting intended to heighten clan tensions, or stoke existing animosities within the community. This meddling need not culminate in armed conflict, only a level of tension sufficient to ensure that a militia leader retains his importance to his clan.

Of the many warlords who engage in this practice, none was as successful in the 1990s as General Mohamed Said Hersi 'Morgan', the son-in-law of the deposed ruler Siyad Barre. Morgan is widely held responsible for war crimes committed against the Isaaq clan during government operations against the Somali National Movement (SNM) in Hargeisa in 1988; a memo he wrote to Barre detailing policies to 'liquidate' what he called 'the Isaaq problem' was leaked, and is now part of an extensive human-rights dossier implicating him in genocidal attacks.[4] No government which ever hopes to cajole the Isaaq into reconsidering secessionism and reuniting Somaliland into a single Somali state can have Morgan at the table; he is a poison pill. He is also likely to be the first individual arrested for war crimes should the Somali people wish to go down that route following the re-establishment of a central government. His own clan, the Mijerteen, distrusts him and most would like to have little to do with him. But Morgan managed to hold the strategic southern port city of Kismayo for nearly all of the 1990s, keeping both external enemies and clan rivals at bay. To do this, he continually fomented animosity between the two largest indigenous clans in the Kismayo area, the Harti (of which the Mijerteen is the largest sub-clan) and the Absame. The Harti and Absame had for over a century quarrelled over pasture and commerce in the Kismayo hinterland, but had also developed well-established mechanisms of conflict management and cooperation. They intermarried, shared important commercial interests and even acquired a regional identity which transcended the clan, calling themselves the 'Waamo group' (*reer Waamo*) after a large seasonal lake in the area. Were the 'Waamo group' to have reconciled, Morgan would not have been able to remain in control of Kismayo. His ability to manipulate tensions within this group, and play third parties (especially the Marehan clan of his father-in-law) off against the Absame and Harti, succeeded in keeping Kismayo in a state of perpetual tension and instability until he was finally driven out in 1999.

Economic interests can also perpetuate tensions. Green lines in Somalia often divide important commercial arteries. On the surface, this would seem to be bad for business, but in fact it creates new business opportunities. Goods are free to pass across green lines, but the trucks carrying them are often vulnerable to theft. In such situations, green lines are the site of large off-loading operations, with goods transferred from truck to truck. Truck owners from some clans have a vested interest in this practice, as it ensures a demand for their services which would not exist were vehicles able to travel safely. Donkey-cart owners, porters and even river-boat operators develop a business interest in the off-loading and reloading which green lines require.

Interests promoting lawlessness

The interests served by an ongoing state of lawlessness in Somalia have also changed over time. During the 1990s, grassroots elements gradually asserted greater control over the young gunmen from their own clans, and clan elders recaptured their traditional role in enforcing customary law and managing disputes. Young gunmen (*mooryaan*), who once wore T-shirts emblazoned with the slogan 'I am the boss', can no longer make that claim, and are much more likely to be held accountable by their own clan for their crimes. Indeed, the social status of young Somali gunmen has plunged – *mooryaan* now inspire disdain, not awe, and far fewer young men are taking up the occupation. As business opportunities and interests have changed, from an economy of plunder to one based mainly on trans-regional and cross-border commerce and a service economy sustained by remittances, business groups at all levels now have a much greater interest in promoting a predictable, safe environment free of militia checkpoints, carjackings and theft. The break which leading Mogadishu businessmen made with warlords in 1999 – when they refused to pay 'taxes' to the militia leaders, and instead bought the militiamen away from the warlords and sub-contracted the management of the militia to sharia courts – was the moment when the business community realised that a certain level of security had to be assured as a 'public good', especially in open roads for commerce. It was also a clear indication that the businessmen were confident that they would win a showdown with the warlords, with whom their interests were increasingly divergent.[5]

The business class has, however, focused on a narrow range of crime for elimination or control. The sharia courts and militia addressed street crime – they kept the seaport town of Merka safe, patrolled the main road between Merka and the warehouses at Bakara market in Mogadishu, and improved security from theft in south Mogadishu. They did not and could not address the Somali equivalent of 'white-collar crime'. This highlights the fact that 'rule of law' and impunity from the law can exist at several levels. Some of the most powerful constituencies in Somalia are served by a rule of law which controls criminality by the underclass, but not a system which has the regulatory, investigatory and enforcement capacity to address 'meta-criminality' – war crimes, the incitement of communal violence, the expropriation of land and buildings, forced labour, the distribution of counterfeit currency, money laundering, piracy, drug smuggling, the illegal export of charcoal and the embezzlement of foreign aid and tax money.[6] The local sharia courts fit this limited legal role well, which is one reason why they will probably re-emerge. For the regulation and prosecution of the kinds of crime committed by some political and economic leaders, a functional state with an autonomous judiciary and police capacity is needed.

Some constituencies are threatened even by the narrow scope of the sharia courts, and so work to undermine efforts to build the rule of law locally. Gangs of bandits and gunmen clearly stand to lose from the enforcement of laws against theft and extortion. Gunmen making a living by providing security to international agencies and wealthy businessmen would find their source of income threatened. Some warlords may quietly work to undermine sharia courts because they represent a rival political force, and because even the modest level of administration that they provide exposes the absence of administration under the warlords.[7] These groups represent only a small percentage of the population, but they have often proved an effective veto coalition against local efforts to impose the rule of law. This is usually done by undermining local confidence in the sharia courts, and typically involves the manipulation of clannism and, sometimes, collusion between rival gangs or militias whose animosity towards one another is set aside in common cause against a greater threat. They are one of the reasons why criminality and extortion continue to plague much of southern Somalia.

Interests promoting state collapse

This is where 'war economy' theories are weakest. If the most powerful interests in Somalia were to pursue their best interests rationally (in the sense of seeking optimal outcomes), then we would expect to see a scenario other than complete state collapse. We would instead predict collusion among the country's economic and political elite to produce a 'paper state' – a government declared and established with the express purpose of attracting foreign aid and other external financial benefits which accrue to recognised states, but without any of the functional capacities expected of such a government. This would dramatically increase the 'spoils of sovereignty' – World Bank loans, property rental to diplomatic missions, and so on – which well-placed elites would enjoy. But the government would lack not only the capacity but, more importantly, the will, to enforce rule of law at a level which could threaten the illicit activities of this elite. The paper state would allow Somalia's economic and political leadership to enjoy all the benefits of a central state without any of the encumbrances.

This may in fact have been the motive behind the effort to establish the TNG in 2000. Nearly all of the political energies devoted to the Arta process which culminated in the creation of the TNG focused on a division of anticipated spoils – namely, the proportion of seats in the parliament and cabinet. Once the TNG was established, virtually all subsequent political energy was geared to courting foreign aid. Very little attention was paid to the actual administration of the country – or, more precisely, those portions of Mogadishu which the TNG controlled. This appeared to many observers a straightforward blueprint for a paper state. For many of the top businessmen and politicians involved in the Arta process, the TNG was in essence a mechanism for luring foreign aid, which could then be diverted.[8] The gambit ultimately failed, in that the TNG never received much bilateral recognition, but it succeeded in netting enough aid (roughly $50m over two years, mainly from Gulf Arab states) to make it a worthwhile venture for some. In fact, domestic and international anger over allegations in June 2001 that millions of dollars of foreign aid provided to the TNG was pocketed by top figures led to the ousting of Prime Minister Ali Khalif Galayr.[9] Reports of inflated contracts for business supporters further soured public confidence.

Ironically, the main objective of the TNG – attracting foreign aid – also sowed the seeds of its failure. The most promising source of foreign aid was the Gulf states. This was immediately recognised by the TNG leadership, which within a month of its establishment called for an 'Arab Marshall Plan' for Somalia. But courting aid from the Gulf states guaranteed that Ethiopia would view the TNG as an unacceptable beachhead for anti-Ethiopian Islamism in the Horn, and would exercise its 'veto' by supporting anti-TNG elements. During 2001, Ethiopian-backed militias and factions blocked TNG efforts to extend its presence beyond parts of Mogadishu, leading to a loss of confidence in the TNG within a year of its declaration.

Elements inside Somalia also worked to undermine the TNG, including some who in theory stood to gain from a successful central state. This suggests the possibility that even had Ethiopia acquiesced, internal interests in Somalia would probably have doomed the initiative. Some political groups – the Puntland leadership, for example – opposed the Arta process because it was structured around criteria for representation which worked against regional administrations. Others opposed the TNG when it became clear that they would not receive leadership positions. Still others became obstructionist because doing so won them valuable support from Ethiopia.

A fourth set of actors appears to have undermined the TNG not because it would work against their interests, but because it threatened to change their operating environment in ways which made it difficult to predict the impact on business and politics. For Mogadishu businessmen who made their fortunes in a setting of complete state collapse, the transition to an environment of state governance – even if a paper state – proved too risky to accept.[10] For the businessmen operating the natural (beach) port facilities at El Ma'an in north Mogadishu, for instance, a state authority reopening the main Mogadishu seaport would be bound to hurt their business. Even offers from the TNG to that business group to manage the Mogadishu port were turned down, despite its lucrative potential. Other business interests are alleged to have undermined the TNG by supporting anti-TNG elements, even while publicly voicing commitment to it for fear that it might evolve and assume capacities which could end illicit business, or tax them without delivering basic security and services in return. These rumours, though almost impossible to verify, were the subject of intense discussion and speculation among the informed Somali public in the summer of 2002.[11] Behaviour such as this can only be understood as risk-averse in an environment of considerable uncertainty. It is not irrational, but rather 'bounded rationality' – a willingness to seek sub-optimal but acceptable outcomes rather than face the risks a revived state would entail. State collapse may be unpalatable, inconvenient and undesirable on any number of counts, but for political and economic actors who have survived and thrived in a stateless setting, embracing a state-building agenda appears to constitute a leap of faith they are unwilling to take.

Chapter 3

Somalia, Global Security and the War on Terrorism

Prior to 11 September 2001, external interest in Somalia's prolonged crisis was mainly humanitarian. The famine of 1991–92 attracted a massive emergency relief presence in the south of the country, culminating in the ill-fated UNOSOM peacekeeping intervention in 1993–95. Following the departure of UNOSOM in March 1995, the world largely disengaged from Somalia, expressing disenchantment with its intractable political crisis and fatigue with its endless need for assistance. What modest attention continued to be given to Somalia remained almost entirely in the realm of humanitarian and rehabilitation aid. Somalia's continued anarchy did raise some security concerns in the 1990s, but those were not accorded serious and sustained attention until 11 September. With no embassies in the country, Western governments monitored political events from distant Nairobi. Few assets were devoted to the task; most embassies in Nairobi had at most a single desk officer following Somalia, and then often as one part of a multi-country assignment. Within the aid community, the high turnover of staff and lack of access to much of the country due to insecurity meant that few international officials could speak authoritatively on security and political matters inside Somalia.

Since the onset of the war on terrorism, however, Somalia has come under intensive scrutiny as a potential safe haven for terrorist networks. Its Islamic movement, Al-Ittihad al-Islamiyya (AIAI), has been the focus of attention for possible links with al-Qaeda. This chapter assesses the security threats posed by Somalia's triple crises of collapsed central government, lawlessness and armed conflict.

What kinds of security threats does the country pose to the outside world? How might terrorist groups – particularly radical Islamic groups – seek to exploit Somalia's collapsed state?

Security concerns prior to 11 September

Even before 11 September, collapsed states had begun to attract attention as potential security threats, both to neighbouring states and to the international community. For adjacent countries, collapsed states threatened to produce a range of destabilising 'spillover' effects – refugees, crime, arms and drug trafficking and warfare itself. This led to concerns about local crises developing into 'regional brushfires' potentially destabilising entire subcontinents. Western interests, it was argued, were hurt by this regional spillover. In 1994, for example, the director of the US Agency for International Development, J. Brian Atwood, argued for engagement in collapsed states on the grounds that 'disintegrating societies and states with their civil conflicts and destabilizing refugee flows have emerged as the greatest menace to global stability'.[1] Containment, once aimed at stemming the tide of communist expansion, was now invoked to halt the spread of anarchy.

Analysts seeking to widen conventional definitions of national security focused on collapsed states as a global as well as a regional threat. There were two variations on this attempt to 'securitise' complex emergencies. One school of thought emphasised the use of collapsed states as safe havens for terrorists and transnational criminal networks. This had a certain appeal to traditional security analysts, as it continued to focus on the threat of physical attack, albeit from non-state actors. A second school of thought focused on new, unconventional security issues, such as the spread of dangerous new strains of disease and environmental degradation.[2] This was considerably harder to sell to national security establishments, though some European capitals took the issue more seriously than did Washington. What all these arguments had in common was a shared conviction that collapsed states were not a direct security threat to countries outside their immediate vicinity, but were rather catalysts, havens and incubators of other threats.[3]

Somalia in the 1990s produced almost all of these security problems for its neighbours and the world, and indeed continues to do so. Spillover from the prolonged crisis has been a matter of urgency for the entire Horn of Africa, as well as Yemen. Kenya suffers particularly in this regard. Hundreds of thousands of Somali refugees have fled to Kenya since 1990, and with few exceptions have stayed there. Poorer Somali households remain in refugee camps in Dadaab (near the Somali border) or Kakuma (near Sudan). Somalis with sources of income live in sprawling neighbourhoods and ghettos in Nairobi, or in towns in the Somali-inhabited portion of north-east Kenya. While most of the refugees are law-abiding, some have introduced a wave of crime into Kenya.

Some of this criminality – such as smuggling – is relatively benign, albeit costly in terms of lost customs revenue to Kenya. Somalis have taken over much of the import–export business by smuggling goods such as sugar and other consumer commodities from Somali beach ports[4] – where goods pass untaxed – across southern Somalia and over the Kenyan border, where they sell for less than the same goods passing through the corrupt and inefficient port of Mombasa. Somalis even engage in arbitrage, purchasing duty-free Kenyan cigarettes, shipping them to Somalia and then trucking them overland back into Kenya. Corrupt customs officials on the Kenyan border are often the only 'tax' these goods ever encounter. Most of the Kenyan–Somali border is unpoliced and well beyond the capacity of the Kenyan government to control. This lucrative transit trade has been a major factor in the rise of the 'entrepot' economy in Mogadishu. One of the unintended consequences of the collapse of the state is that it has rendered Somalia the largest duty-free shop in the world, a fact which Somali merchants have been quick to exploit.[5]

Other aspects of criminality associated with Somali refugees have had grave effects on Kenyan security. The flow of small arms into Kenya has been especially destabilising. Some studies have estimated the volume of arms entering Kenya from Somalia at up to 5,000 automatic rifles per month.[6] Clashes over land and pasture are now far more violent and bloody, approaching wartime casualty rates in parts of the country.[7] Criminal groups in Nairobi are generally better armed than the police – except in instances when the police themselves are forming the criminal gangs. Somali bandits roam freely into north-eastern Kenya, and have been implicated in cattle raids as far south as northern Tanzania. The clannism and violence of Somali refugees have infected the Kenyan Somali population, politicising lineage identities to a degree not known in the past. Somali Kenyan Members of Parliament (MPs) all possess their own private militias thanks in large part to the violence brought by Somali refugees. Moreover, Kenya has lost control over a good portion of the north-eastern hinterland; armed convoys are required for overland travel to border towns and refugee camps, and for most of the 1990s the Kenyan side of the border was generally more lawless and dangerous than the Somali side. This lawlessness has found its way into the heart of Nairobi. The teeming Somali slum of Eastleigh has become a virtual no-go zone for the Kenyan authorities, a world unto itself where black-market activity is rife, criminals can slip away undetected and guns can be rented by the day.[8] Whole sections of north-eastern towns such as Mandera and Garissa are off-limits to the Kenyan police and military after dark, and the refugee camps at Dadaab – host to over 100,000 refugees – are also impenetrable. It is important not to overstate Somalia's contribution to Kenya's notorious criminality – Kenyan officials are inclined to scapegoat Somalis for all of the country's crime and insecurity woes – but it is clearly true that Somalia has significantly exacerbated a crisis of lawlessness which costs Kenya unknown amounts in lost business, lost tourism and lost human lives. The arms flow from Somalia also raises stakes in inter-ethnic tensions inside Kenya, increasing the chances that some of these conflicts could spin out of control. In the wake of two major terrorist attacks in Kenya – the 1998 bombing of the US embassy in Nairobi and the December 2002 attack on a tourist hotel in Mombasa – Kenya's government has, with US military assistance, made serious efforts to patrol its border areas more vigorously. This will eventually contain at least some of the spillover from Somalia, but it will take time.

Somalia has also produced a number of global security problems. The country has been an incubator for two serious diseases which have spread beyond its borders, one a threat to humans (drug-resistant tuberculosis), the other a threat to both humans and livestock (Rift Valley Fever). Rift Valley Fever, a vector-borne disease which mosquitoes can transmit from infected livestock to humans, was detected in livestock exported out of Somalia into Saudi Arabia in September 2000; it led to an outbreak which claimed the lives of over 100 Saudis.[9] This prompted the re-imposition of a ban on Somali livestock imports by the Gulf states, which has been devastating to Somalia's pastoral economy, as livestock is the country's chief export. Other pandemics could easily erupt given the ideal circumstances inside Somalia. The widespread misuse of pharmaceutical drugs, which are freely sold in market kiosks, is creating conditions ripe for the development of drug-resistant strains of disease. The collapse of sanitation, combined with crowded conditions and a shortage of clean water in towns and camps for internally displaced people (IDPs), encourages the rapid spread of disease.[10] The collapse of government health and veterinary services, combined with chronic insecurity, makes it extremely difficult for international health agencies such as the World Health Organisation (WHO) and the UN Children's Fund (UNICEF) to conduct vaccination campaigns and monitor outbreaks of disease.[11] The high volume of out-migration and the global distribution of Somalia's refugee population mean that any outbreak of a new or highly resistant disease in Somalia is likely to travel quickly abroad. International health officials express concern that Somalia's ongoing crisis may produce such an epidemic, but to date this has not happened. No cases of Ebola have been reported there, and the AIDS epidemic which is ravaging Kenya and Ethiopia has been slower to spread inside Somalia.[12]

Narcotic drug production and trafficking, often associated with failed states such as Myanmar, Afghanistan and Colombia, have been much less of a problem in Somalia. There are persistent reports of marijuana production in southern Somalia and its shipment into Kenya, but available evidence suggests that this is a relatively minor activity. Environmental security threats emanating from Somalia are more serious. Companies have exploited Somalia's unpatrolled coastline to dump toxic waste; in some instances they have reached deals with local warlords to do so in the Somali interior. Another environmental issue is the unregulated harvesting of Somalia's acacia forests for charcoal, which fetches high prices in the Gulf states. The resulting deforestation is producing dramatic erosion, reducing the carrying capacity of the rangelands. Acacia harvesting in the south of Somalia, exported out of Kismayo, is reaching the Kenyan border. Charcoal exports were illegal under the former government, but are now completely unregulated. Profits from the trade are controlled by businessmen close to the TNG in Mogadishu and the Jubba Valley Alliance (JVA), which runs Kismayo port, so that even if these local authorities had the capacity to regulate the trade (which they do not) they have no interest in stopping it.

The outflow of Somali refugees and illegal immigrants from

Somalia to Europe, North America, Australia and the Gulf has constituted one of the most vexing political problems emanating from Somalia's collapse. Although primarily a political rather than a security concern, Somalia's estimated million-strong diaspora has been a major preoccupation for host countries. Members of the diaspora play a vital role in keeping the Somali economy afloat, sending back remittances estimated to amount to $500m per year, by far the largest source of hard currency in the country.[13] Without that infusion of cash, Somalia would be unable to sustain its modest consumption levels and would be an even bigger humanitarian crisis than it already is. In the long term, however, the remittance economy is dangerously unsustainable, and the diaspora itself robs Somalia of the professionals it needs to rebuild.

For host countries, the role of the diaspora in the Somali economy is incidental to the more immediate political complications some Somali immigrants create.[14] In Canada, for instance, Somali clan disputes have erupted into violence, and young Somalis have formed gangs. The strong cultural identity Somalis possess makes them relatively disinclined to assimilate, producing ethnic enclaves in countries which are not always accustomed to this as a feature of their urban landscape. Some Somalis exploit generous family reunification policies for refugees by fraudulently claiming nephews and even non-relatives as children (often for a fee).[15] All this in turn has created public resentment against Somali communities, fuelling a rise in support for anti-immigrant right-wing and neo-fascist movements from Canada to Scandinavia. For some of these countries, finding a solution to Somalia's collapsed state is an urgent matter not for reasons of national security, but rather so that they can justify repatriating Somalis.

Somalia's long unpatrolled coastline is the scene of two international criminal activities – illegal fishing by foreign vessels, which is depleting the marine life off the coast, and piracy, conducted by Somali marine militias against foreign yachts, fishing trawlers and commercial ships. Piracy off Somalia's north-eastern coast is endemic, prompting the International Maritime Bureau to increase its rating of the risk of attack along the Somali coastline from 'possibility' to 'certainty'.[16] Because pirates often kidnap crews for ransom, this criminal activity creates considerable diplomatic difficulties for the countries of the nationals being held, and in one instance nearly provoked a military response from France.

The greatest worry of international observers is the potential use of Somalia as a safe haven by terrorists. This has been expressed almost exclusively in terms of Islamic terrorist threats, an issue which receives separate treatment below. But non-Islamic terrorist organisations can also conceivably exploit Somalia as a safe haven. In fact (depending on how one distinguishes between terrorist group and liberation front), this has arguably already occurred. The Oromo Liberation Front (OLF) used Somalia as a base for attacks against the Ethiopian government for several years in the mid-1990s. Ethiopia's subsequent efforts to build up Somali clients in border areas and its occasional incursions across the border have ended OLF activities there.

Terrorism and political Islamic movements in the 1990s

A final security concern which emerged in Somalia in the 1990s was the threat posed by radical Islam. For the most part, worries that Islamists would take over pockets of the collapsed country, or even come to exercise control over the entire state, were decoupled from concerns that Somalia would be used as a terrorist safe haven. The link between Islamist movements and terrorist threats has grown incrementally, driven by a series of attacks in neighbouring states in which Somalis or Somalia played an important role.

There are several distinct threats which radical Islam may pose in Somalia. The first is the negative impact of ascendant political Islam as an alternative system of governance. Islamist groups which exploit Somali collapse to gain control over ports, towns, regional administrations or judiciaries are a fundamental challenge to progress in democratisation, modernisation and human rights. Islam as a system of governance, even if peaceful and not involved in terrorism, is thus seen in some quarters as a threat to broader Western interests, something to tolerate in Saudi Arabia, but not to encourage elsewhere. Somalis with a more secular inclination are most forceful in advancing this argument, but this position has wide support outside the country as well, where opposition to political Islam is often an article of faith. A second concern is over the possibility of Somali Islamists engaging in direct acts of terrorism. This was not a major preoccupation until a series of assassination attempts and bombings against the Ethiopian government in Addis Ababa in 1996, carried out by the Somali Islamist organisation,

Al-Ittihad al-Islami (AIAI). A third category of concern is over Somali Islamists providing assistance to transnational Islamic terrorists. This aid can range from the facilitation of financial transfers to hosting terrorist training camps to harbouring al-Qaeda members. How realistic these threats are is explored below.

The principal Islamic organisation in Somalia, initially known as the Muslim Brotherhood and eventually as AIAI, emerged in the 1980s as one of at least seven different Islamist movements in Mogadishu.[17] AIAI was comprised mainly of educated young men who had studied or worked in the Middle East. They came to the conclusion that the only way to rid Somalia of the corruption, repression and tribalism of the Barre years was via political Islam. In this sense, AIAI mirrored many Islamic movements in the Middle East. The movement accounted for a very small segment of the community; Somali society has historically been averse to the more puritanical strains of Wahhabism associated with Saudi Islamic practices. Most Somalis view Wahhabism as a foreign ideology. The Islamists faced opposition from many quarters – from the state, traditional sheikhs, clan elders and the bulk of the population. In 1990, few considered political Islam to be a movement of any consequence.[18]

When the opposition forces which overthrew the Barre regime were unable to agree on power-sharing in a new government and the country plunged into protracted civil war, Al-Ittihad sought to take advantage, mainly by attempting to seize 'targets of opportunity' – strategic sites such as seaports and commercial crossroads. In 1991, they attempted to hold the northern seaport of Bosaso, but were driven out by the Mijerteen Somali Salvation Democratic Front (SSDF), sustaining heavy casualties in the process. In the more chaotic south, Islamists controlled and ran the seaports at Kismayo and Merka for much of 1991 before warlords pushed them out. There, the movement impressed international relief agencies with its honesty – in sharp contrast to the faction leaders, who used control of the ports to divert food aid and extort relief agencies. For their part, the faction leaders and warlords viewed the Islamists as a greater threat than rival militias, not because of AIAI's military power – it was quite weak – but because its responsible approach to port administration, and its relatively functional cohesiveness as a local organisation, exposed the factions' indifference and incompetence. The Islamists tended to organise within rather than across clan lines, so that clan-based factions viewed them as dangerous internal rivals. Al-Ittihad grew more threatening to the factions as the violence and lawlessness dragged on, because it promised unity, justice and – most importantly – the rule of law in a country seriously deficient in all three. Given the carnage and chaos of 1991–92, what is surprising is not that an Islamist movement emerged, but that it was not able to garner more popular support than it did. Even in such desperate conditions, Somalis remained suspicious of politically active Islam and remained attached to the clan as the sole source of protection.

In only one location did Al-Ittihad manage to maintain sustained control of territory. From 1991 to 1996, it governed the town of Luuq and its environs in the south-western region of Gedo, near the border with Ethiopia and Kenya. Its tenure in Luuq, a small but important commercial town, provided important clues about a movement that otherwise has been largely the subject of speculation.[19] One lesson was that AIAI wins public support mainly by providing responsive administration and, above all, the effective rule of law. Residents of Luuq recall law and order as the chief virtue of the Islamic administration; businesses were especially appreciative as the low crime rate facilitated commerce. This pattern of public response to sharia law occurs in the mid-to-late 1990s in Mogadishu and elsewhere in south-central Somalia. But public appreciation for Islamic rule declines quickly when Islamists attempt to intrude too far into social matters. The Islamists in Luuq and elsewhere struggled unsuccessfully, against clannism in particular. In the end, Islamic rule in Luuq was embedded within clan customs and rule, rather than superseding them. This too has become a prevailing pattern for Islamists throughout the country.

The administration of Luuq under the Islamists was strict. An 'Islamic Association' exercised overall authority, beneath which a district council, appointed by the Islamic Association, handled day-to-day management. A sharia court administered justice based on Islamic law rather than customary clan law or *xeer*; this meant that punishments included amputation, which is not at all customary in Somalia, though some other Somali sharia courts have imposed it, notably in north Mogadishu. The police force was composed of Islamic militia but kept separate from the security forces. Consumption of the mild narcotic leaf *qaat*, a popular habit, was forbidden, as was cultivation of tobacco. Veiling was enforced on women. Free education was provided in schools, but courses were taught in Arabic and the curriculum was Islamic, not secular, in orientation.

Most of the core leadership of AIAI in Luuq was from a dominant local clan, the Marehan, but over time Luuq attracted AIAI members from other clans. On the one hand, this demonstrated AIAI's commitment to overcoming clannism. On the other, the presence of outside clans was seized upon by the secular Marehan faction in the region, the SNF, to claim that Al-Ittihad was a 'foreign front' taking control of Marehan land. This forced AIAI into the awkward position of insisting that it was Marehan, even as it embraced the notion that its members 'had no clan but Islam'. Worse, because Luuq town and district is shared by other clans, the more Al-Ittihad claimed it was Marehan, the more it alienated non-Marehan residents, who came to view it as just another manifestation of Marehan hegemony. This struggle to reconcile a universalist identity and ideology with the powerful, parochial forces of Somali clannism has remained a major challenge for the AIAI.

From a narrow law and order perspective, AIAI in Luuq unquestionably provided a much safer environment than almost any other region of Somalia enjoyed during the turbulent and anarchic period of 1991–92. International agencies were able to work there, and some found the fundamentalists preferable to deal with – more professional, better able to maintain security, less likely to extort. Luuq hospital, which was administered by AIAI, was frequently cited as a model of good organisation and accountability at a time when virtually all hospitals in Somalia were plagued by corruption and theft. According to a 1994 African Medical and Research Foundation (AMREF) report:

> *working in Luuq district, security is not a major issue – the district benefits from the good security which is the result of strict administration by the Islamic Association. However, most implementing agencies working in other districts of Gedo still face problems of intimidation, kidnapping, theft, and violence.*[20]

Even the Kenyan military and police authorities at the border town of Mandera expressed a preference for Al-Ittihad administration over the SNM faction in the adjacent district of Bulo Hawa, noting that security always improved when the AIAI controlled the area. This was, however, offset by profound discomfort in Western circles with the sharia code of punishments, the treatment of women and other practices, which were criticised as violations of human rights.

One of the most revealing aspects about Al-Ittihad in Luuq (and in Gedo region more broadly) was its source of local support. In 1991, the regionally-dominant Marehan clan was composed of two groups – the local inhabitants (known as the *guri*), and newcomers or guests (*galti*) from Mogadishu and central Somalia, seeking safe haven in Gedo during the civil war. The *galti*, who included many powerful, wealthy ex-members of the Barre regime, dominated the Marehan SNF faction. Resentment against the *galti* among Marehan clansmen native to Gedo was palpable. This tended to manifest itself in strong support for Al-Ittihad by the *guri*, which viewed Al-Ittihad as a viable opposition force against the *galti*-dominated SNF. Divisions within the Marehan clan over Al-Ittihad could by no means be reduced to this *guri–galti* tension, but it was a significant factor. This anecdotal evidence suggests that Somalis may gravitate towards Islamist movements for a wide range of reasons, some local and pragmatic, rather than global and ideological.

The Islamic authorities in Luuq were forced to deal with the same contentious clan issues as other types of administration, and were not above clannish behaviour themselves. The Islamist security forces were composed mainly of young gunmen whose devotion to the tenets of fundamentalist Islam was negligible, and who fought in the name of AIAI only because Al-Ittihad paid them. This was no *mujahideen*, no corps of ideologically committed zealots willing to fight and die for the cause. They engaged in extortion, threats and other behaviour comparable to gunmen in secular factions, and Al-Ittihad was not always in a position to control them. The imposition of strict sharia law and the outlawing of *qaat* were not well-received by most residents. In the end, despite the appreciation many residents had for the peace and security Al-Ittihad delivered, the public in Luuq did not resist the Ethiopian military offensive that drove the group out in 1996.[21]

One accusation levelled at AIAI in Luuq caught the attention of US and UN officials during the UNOSOM peace operation in 1993–94. Some international aid officials based in Luuq claimed that

Arab visitors periodically arrived by light aircraft as guests of the Islamic administration. Because Al-Ittihad rejected the peace operation, no UNOSOM military or civilian officials were based in Luuq or even cleared to visit, so that only a limited number of foreign aid workers had first-hand knowledge of the situation there. Rumours of Sudanese support for AIAI in Luuq circulated, and given the politics of Sudan and its frosty relations with Ethiopia at the time seemed entirely plausible. This prompted speculation that Luuq was being supported or used by foreign Islamic radicals.

The Islamist experiment in Luuq ended abruptly in 1996, when the town was attacked by Ethiopian forces and the Islamists dispersed. The move was a response to the string of assassination attempts and bombings by Al-Ittihad in Addis Ababa. It is unclear if Ethiopia was convinced that Al-Ittihad was using Luuq as a base of operations, or if it was simply taking precautionary measures against a potential threat on its border. Marehan members of Al-Ittihad later reorganised as the 'Islamic Group of Gedo Region', emphasising their regional identity so as to distance themselves from the Ethiopian Al-Ittihad movement, as well as the Islamist groups responsible for the bombing of the US embassy in Nairobi in 1998. The Islamic Group of Gedo Region argued that it had nothing to do with AIAI attacks in Ethiopia, and was furious at the AIAI branch inside Ethiopia for resorting to terrorist tactics, as Luuq bore the brunt of Ethiopia's retaliation.[22] It is difficult to confirm whether this claim is accurate or simply a public-relations move, but given Somalia's fractious clannism the idea that AIAI would also encounter regional and clan schisms makes intuitive sense.

Al-Ittihad learned from its experience in Luuq, and made significant adjustments to its strategy after 1996. First, it concluded that, for the time being, it had to work within the logic of Somali clannism rather than attempting to transcend it – cross-clan coalitions were too easily exploited by factional adversaries. The movement was already decentralised along lineage lines; the experience at Luuq pushed that decentralisation further. Since 1996, Al-Ittihad cells have worked almost entirely autonomously at the clan and sub-clan level. Splits within the leadership have fuelled the tendency towards fragmentation – two of the best known AIAI figures, Hassan Turki and Hassan Dahir Aweys, are known to be fierce rivals.[23] Second, the attack on Luuq underscored that a strategy aimed at holding territory was counter-productive; it only provided adversaries such as Ethiopia with easy fixed targets to attack. In response, AIAI adopted a strategy of integrating into local communities rather than standing apart from them. Today, AIAI members are teachers, businessmen, journalists and other fully integrated members of local communities.

Third, the movement concluded that clannish Somalia was not yet ready for Islamic rule, and opted instead for a long-term strategy of educating and preparing Somali society, with an emphasis on Islamic education. This entailed establishing or expanding Islamic schools and relief centres, usually through external Islamic aid agencies, which possessed the funding to provide quality schooling (in Arabic, and often with Egyptian teachers), free food and other benefits. The provision of services to desperately poor communities has won local support. Arabic-language instruction is valued as a potential way out of Somalia to work in the Gulf. This tactic has made it difficult to distinguish between those Islamic activists who are committed to a relatively apolitical project of deeper Islamisation of Somali society (the agenda of the al-Islah movement, via Islamic aid agencies sponsored by the Saudi government), and those groups that are using Islamic NGOs and schools to further a more overt political agenda. The fact that Saudi and other externally sponsored programmes are not well-monitored by their donors makes it harder to know when such NGOs have been infiltrated by groups with radical political aims. Yet distinguishing between al-Islah and Al-Ittihad is imperative, lest legitimate Islamic aid agencies come to be seen in the same light as Al-Ittihad.[24]

AIAI also prepares for the long term by building a strong economic base (its members have entered business and have sought to recruit businessmen) and by gaining influence in key sectors shaping Somali society, in particular the media and local judiciaries. Some of the remittance or *hawilaad* companies have been accused of ties to Al-Ittihad, though hard evidence has been difficult to secure.

In addition, Al-Ittihad has forged alliances of expedience with secular Somali political groupings, rather than opposing them outright. This has given it opportunities to increase its activities and influence locally. These marriages of convenience are usually born of the logic 'the enemy of my enemy is my friend'. In Somalia, this typically means that a faction or other political grouping which finds itself in hostile relations with Ethiopia is more receptive to working with Al-Ittihad, to gain access to whatever external resources the movement may be in a position to secure. Faction leaders have been notoriously fickle on this score. The Mogadishu warlord Hussein Aideed (son of deceased General Mohamed Farah Aideed, who fought US and UN troops in 1993) at times flirted with Al-Ittihad, but then accused the TNG of being a front for radical Islamists. Aideed and his faction are now allies of Ethiopia.[25]

Finally, in some parts of Somalia al-Ittihad has adopted what can loosely be called the 'Turabi' strategy. That is, rather than making an outright bid for power over local administrations, it seeks instead to gain control over key branches of that administration (such as the judiciary), while a secular authority presides over the administration as a whole. This allows Al-Ittihad to promote an Islamic agenda and build a political base while remaining largely unseen. Ideally, it hopes to achieve what Hassan al Turabi succeeded in doing for a time in Sudan – gradually outmanoeuvring a civilian government and indirectly controlling politics without ever claiming direct control of the administration. The most notable attempt to implement this strategy was in Puntland, where Islamists succeeded in winning control of the Ministry of Justice even though the leadership of President Abdullahi Yusuf was strongly opposed to AIAI. Concerns about the influence of Al-Ittihad in the TNG in Mogadishu were based on the presumption that the same strategy was being applied there. Some observers feel that the Islamists are more likely to infiltrate and eventually control political structures established by others than attempt to establish such structures themselves.[26]

The result of the devolution of AIAI in Somalia is that the organisation has taken on very different features in different parts of the country. In Ethiopia, AIAI is considered a terrorist organisation due to its involvement in the bombings and assassination attempts of 1996.[27] In Somaliland, Islamists are politically quiescent. In Gedo, the Islamic Group has actively sought out cooperative relations with international aid organisations and attempted to position itself as moderate and non-violent. Al-Ittihad in Puntland has been more strident, anti-Western and organised, but has not been implicated in violence; it has engaged more openly in local politics than have most cells, first by gaining control of the Puntland judiciary and then by supporting Ali Jama Ali in his failed bid to hold power in Puntland. In the lower Jubba region, Islamists have engaged in several assassinations and attacks against Western aid workers, and Islamists in Merka have on occasion attacked the compounds of international aid organisations. In Mogadishu, al-Ittihad enjoyed significant success in building a power base among some of the powerful merchants in the city, and in 1999 was involved in the management of the business-backed sharia militia and court system, which brought a good deal of law and order to south Mogadishu. But Islamists in Mogadishu have suffered missteps in their periodic bids to take more direct political roles. The first occurred in the mid-1990s, when the leader of the sharia courts in north Mogadishu, Ali Dheere, attempted to assert leadership over the entire Abgal clan at the expense of the USC faction; his militia was quickly routed and the sharia courts were dismantled. Al-Ittihad later opted to support the establishment of the TNG, but in the process bargained shamelessly for positions in the administration, leading many to conclude that AIAI members were simply opportunists using the movement to earn a valuable ministerial seat. AIAI was accused of acting like any other faction, and lost a good deal of credibility.

Indeed, AIAI is widely regarded as a spent force, marginal if not defunct as an organisation. It has been unable to hold territory; its ideological appeal has failed to overcome clannist cleavages, forcing to work within, rather than cross, lineage identities; clan and faction leaders have consistently been able to out-manoeuvre it; it lost considerable legitimacy in the eyes of the public through its maladroit political jockeying for positions within the TNG; and its identification by the US government as a terrorist organisation has rendered it a poison chalice in Somalia, conferring few benefits and many liabilities on potential members. It must still be taken seriously as a potentially important political force, should circumstances permit its members to regroup and should external Islamists provide it with financial support. AIAI activities inside Ethiopia, for instance, are still worrisome, and some individual Somali AIAI members are suspected of collaborating with al-Qaeda. But overstating the importance of AIAI runs the risk of blinding observers to other, perhaps more significant trends in political Islam in contemporary Somalia.

Though AIAI has declined in importance, political Islam as a broader movement and sentiment in Somalia is clearly robust and ascendant, attracting growing numbers of people in education, business, and other sectors. The most obvious manifestation of growing Islamist tendencies in Somalia has been the rapid development of an extraordinarily successful social service network in Mogadishu known as al-Islah. Al-Islah is an Islamic charity movement which draws in part on donations from private and official funders in the Gulf states, and in part on local contributions and user fees, to provide some of the best education and hospitals in the country. It has extended support to a network of schools educating 100,000 students in Mogadishu, and also established the University of Mogadishu, which is providing 5,000 students with high quality training in a number of fields. Al-Islah is considered to be a relatively progressive Islamist movement, seeking to deepen Islamic practices and values in Somalia and disavowing any links with AIAI. Its leadership has welcomed contacts with western aid officials, diplomats, and universities. Al-Islah has to date remained a social rather than a political movement, but its extensive networks and its broad support from the public in Mogadishu give it the potential to play a more overt political role if and when it chooses to do so.[28] In 2003, it flexed its political muscles for the first time by calling for strikes at hospitals and schools and organising street protests in response to violent crimes perpetrated by militias. The future political direction that al-Islah takes will likely have a major impact on Somali politics in coming years.

One concern raised about al-Islah is the possibility that some members of AIAI are seeking affiliation with the al-Islah network, as supporters or employees in the hospitals and schools, with the aim of using al-Islah as a Trojan horse within which to regroup and recruit. It is extremely difficult to determine the extent to which this infiltration may or may not be occurring. But in either event, the deepening of Islamic identity which al-Islah promotes could work in the long-term interests of Islamic radicals. There is at this time no evidence that the Islamic schools in Mogadishu are playing a radical recruiting role akin to the madrasses in Pakistan, but they are socialising an entire generation of young Somalis into a worldview that is likely to earn radical Islamic movements more adherents in years to come. Anecdotal evidence of the political views of some of the teachers in these schools suggest that at least some subscribe to very angry, anti-Western, radical, and conspiratorial interpretations of events. This suggests the possibility that the real Islamic threat in Somalia may be in a stage of incubation, likely to manifest itself in ten or 20 years.

Some observers contend that AIAI's members have concluded that Somali society is not yet ready for Islamic rule, leading AIAI members to focus on reintegrating into society and working to educate their communities as teachers, journalists, members of local judiciaries, and in other sensitive positions. If in fact Islamists believe that the goal of bringing Islamic rule to Somalia is a generational project, requiring years of work to prepare Somali society, then the emphasis on education is entirely logical.

The agenda of the Somali Islamists – both al-Islah and Al-Ittihad – has tended to be fairly inward-looking, and relatively disengaged from the international concerns of most other Islamist movements. Somali Islamists are not nearly as invested in the Israeli–Palestinian conflict, for instance, as are their foreign counterparts. An important exception to this rule is AIAI's agenda in Somali-inhabited portions of Ethiopia, where it is committed to bringing Islamic rule.[29] But even there, Ethiopian Somali Islamists appear much more dedicated to the cause than AIAI members inside Somalia itself. Indeed, one by-product of the Somali civil war is a palpable decline in adherence to irredentist claims on Somali-inhabited Ethiopian territory by clans which do not have a significant presence inside Ethiopia. Political figures from the Hawiye clan-family, for instance, proposed at the Kenyan peace talks that only Somalis born inside the country qualify as Somali citizens – a tactic intended to weaken the rival Darood clan-family, many of whose members are in Ethiopia and Kenya.

The most important debate about AIAI, and one which is very difficult to resolve in the absence of firm evidence, is the extent to which the organisation enjoys links to external radical Islamist movements, and the significance of those links. Allegations of extensive and intimate ties between AIAI and al-Qaeda have never been supported by any 'smoking gun' – no Somalis appear in al-Qaeda's top leadership, and until 2003 no Somali was involved in a terrorist plot against a Western target outside of Somalia.[30] As many as 200 Somalis fought in Afghanistan as *mujahideen* in the 1980s and 1990s, but they do not appear to have sustained a subsequent role in al-Qaeda. What appears increasingly clear, however, is that Somali individuals – who may or may not be members of Al-Ittihad – have had dealings with al-Qaeda or al-Qaeda-affiliated companies. Because most major business transactions by Somali merchants transpire in

Dubai, where Osama bin Laden's business empire was active, it is almost certain that some loans and partnerships entered into by Somalis link them with al-Qaeda companies and money. The significance of such business ties is hard to assess. Some are probably incidental, while others may suggest long-term relationships with political implications. Given evidence that at least four non-Somali al-Qaeda suspects have enjoyed safe haven in Mogadishu since 2001, some Somali businessmen and others unquestionably have substantial links to al-Qaeda.[31] But on the whole the Somali business class, and Somali political figures, have long taken a pragmatic and calculating attitude towards external ideologies and power, forging alliances of expediency and then dropping them the moment they constitute a liability. Somalia's effortless shift in the late 1970s from socialism and a treaty of friendship with the Soviet Union to close ties with the West and lip-service to economic liberalisation is a case in point.

Terrorism and radical Islam in Somalia today

Concern that Somalia's Islamist movements might constitute a broader threat to international security first arose in the aftermath of the al-Qaeda-sponsored terrorist attack on the US embassies in Nairobi and Dar es Salaam in August 1998. No Somalis were implicated in the attacks themselves, but evidence pointed to the possibility that Somalia was used as a site for preparations for the attack.[32] Analysts began to reconsider the claims made years earlier by bin Laden that al-Qaeda had directly supported Somali militia in attacks on US peacekeeping forces, including the firefight on 3–4 October 1993 that left 18 US soldiers dead. 'Bin Laden, we now believe, provided training and equipment in the early 1990s to the factional fighters that killed Americans in Mogadishu,' claimed former Assistant Secretary of state for Africa Susan Rice.[33] But most observers saw the claim as an attempt by bin Laden to earn credit for events in which al-Qaeda in fact had no part. The Somali faction fighting the US and UN troops in Mogadishu, the SNA led by Aideed, was strongly opposed to Islamists in Somalia and was thus an unlikely collaborator with al-Qaeda. US and UN officials working in the UNOSOM operation in 1993 concur that al-Qaeda and bin Laden were never known to be operational inside Somalia, though they may have been a minor source of funds or weapons. Somalis are even more emphatic that bin Laden had nothing to do with the armed clashes between UN forces and Aideed's militia.

In the aftermath of the 11 September terrorist attacks on New York and Washington, concerns about terrorist links inside Somalia rose dramatically. As al-Qaeda was attacked and driven from Afghanistan, so Somalia quickly earned a spot on the short-list of countries which might be targeted in an expanded war on terrorism. Initially this was earned not by direct evidence of Islamist radicalism in Somalia, but rather by a process of deduction. Somalia met a number of criteria which made it an obvious 'state of concern': it is an Islamic society; a collapsed state where terrorists could operate beyond the reach of the law; an impoverished land where radicals could easily buy local cooperation; and it had an indigenous political Islamist movement. This placed it in the company of Yemen as possible countries where al-Qaeda members, including bin Laden himself, might seek to relocate. Naval interdiction and patrols of the Somali coast were initiated; aerial surveillance was conducted; and increased intelligence assets were devoted to monitoring a country which had been given little attention since 1994. In October 2001, the US Treasury Department froze the assets of the largest Somali remittance and telecommunications company, al-Barakaat, claiming that it was part of al-Qaeda's global financial empire. The department never provided information to clarify the specific charges against al-Barakaat, and among Somalia analysts the move is widely seen as questionable.[34]

By November 2001, statements from some US government departments – particularly some quarters in the Department of Defense (DoD) – suggested that the US had compelling evidence of an al-Qaeda presence in Somalia. 'Somalia,' said Deputy Defense Secretary Paul Wolfowitz, 'has a certain al Qaeda presence already.'[35] Defense Secretary Donald Rumsfeld claimed that 'Somalia has been a place that has harboured Al-Qaeda and, to my knowledge, still is.'[36] Several distinct charges were levelled. The most serious was that al-Qaeda had a base of operation in Somalia, including training camps. A second claim was that Al-Ittihad was a subsidiary of al-Qaeda, and that the two organisations should be considered synonymous; this placed every Al-Ittihad cell and member at risk. A third charge was that the TNG in Mogadishu was a Trojan horse for Al-Ittihad, the Somali equivalent of the Taliban regime in Afghanistan. In the slippery logic of the day, this meant that some came to view the TNG as an al-Qaeda front.

The media seized on and drove this story, making Somalia a high-profile issue once again. The unequivocal charges from DoD were interspersed with more cautious statements, mainly from the US Department of State (DoS), that Somalia could become a base for terrorists. Somalia was a concern, stated Secretary of State Colin Powell, 'because terrorist activity might find some fertile ground there, and we don't want that to happen'.[37] These inconsistent positions made it apparent that there were divisions inside the US government on the terrorist threat posed by Somalia. Although DoD was most often associated with more hawkish views on Somalia, it too was split on the subject. But for a time, the prevailing view was that Somalia was hosting al-Qaeda cells. Preparations for military operations were made, ranging from missile attacks on suspected bases to snatch operations against individual suspects to the grooming of proxy Somali forces which could mount an attack on al-Qaeda targets. Fears of an imminent attack on the TNG itself caused panic in Mogadishu. Sources inside the US government contend that the Bush administration came close to approving military action in Somalia in January or February 2002.

Some of the most alarmist fears – that al-Qaeda had training camps and bases in Somalia, or that Al-Ittihad was operating as a subsidiary of al-Qaeda – were eventually dispelled as the US stepped up its monitoring and intelligence-gathering. That effort produced no evidence of al-Qaeda bases in Somalia. DoD, which had initially relied uncritically on Ethiopian military intelligence, discovered that the Ethiopians and some of their Somali allies had vested interests in exaggerating the threat of radical Islam in Somalia. Ethiopia was especially eager to paint the TNG as an Islamist front to discredit an administration it viewed as hostile.[38] On closer inspection, the Americans discovered that the TNG was little more than a group of quarrelling politicians unable to exert control even in the neighbourhood across the street from the hotel where they convened. Far from being a terrorist threat, the TNG was simply irrelevant. Alleged terrorist bases in remote coastal areas like Ras Kiamboni proved to be nothing more than the abandoned mud huts of fishing communities. Those Somali individuals known to be AIAI leaders – notably Hassan Turki and Hassan Dahir Aweys – were not considered dangerous enough to warrant the enormous risks of a 'snatch and grab' mission in Mogadishu's heavily-armed warrens.[39] By March 2002, the apparent absence of serious threats and targets in Somalia led to a shift in the US position, and discussions of possible military action were quietly dropped. The country remained the subject of intensive monitoring, including aerial surveillance and naval patrols, but no action inside Somalia was taken.

This overheated American policy towards Somalia from October 2001 to March 2002 provided an early and revealing glimpse into the Bush administration's policymaking process in the expanded war on terrorism. It exposed how little intelligence had been devoted to areas of the world like Somalia, countries which had been dismissed as marginal but which suddenly acquired new significance as potential safe havens for terrorists. The paucity of reliable intelligence produced widely divergent interpretations of the threat of Islamic radicalism. This in turn opened the door for politicised analyses which had little basis in reality, but which enjoyed the decisive advantage of certainty in a context of confusion, and which, in the absence of high-quality information, were difficult to refute. The argument that al-Qaeda was operational in Somalia and that Al-Ittihad was inextricably linked to it won the day, for a time, simply because it was forcefully and confidently articulated by a small set of DoD officials claiming to have access to privileged information. This revealed a second feature of the administration's decision-making – the relatively narrow range of sources and opinions which Rumsfeld's inner circle relied upon to render policy judgements. Had a wider range of opinions about Somalia been solicited and taken seriously, top officials in DoD would never have been so unequivocal in their statements about the Islamist threat in Somalia.

Although initial assessments of the threat of terrorism emanating from Somalia were overblown, the general concern that al-Qaeda could use the country in some manner was not. From 2001 to 2003, evidence began to emerge that terrorist activities inside Somalia were in fact in a state of evolution. A review of the four major terrorist acts associated with Somalia or Somalis demonstrates this.

The first acts of terrorism associated with Somalia were the attacks in Ethiopia in 1996, which were attributed to Al-Ittihad. These attacks – consisting of assassinations attempts and a hotel bombing – eventually earned AIAI a place on the US list of terrorist organisations. But the 1996 incidents were perpetrated by Somalis of

Ethiopian citizenship, and in the name of a local, not a global, cause – the demand for Islamic government in Somali-inhabited territory of Ethiopia and Somalia. In some ways, AIAI's agenda was not all that distinct from the irredentist claims on the Ogaden region by secular Somali nationalists.

In August 1998, al-Qaeda operatives bombed the US embassies in Nairobi and Dar es Salaam. Although no Somalis were involved in the attacks themselves, Somalia was used as a transit point for bomb material, and after the attacks at least two suspects in the bombings, including the mastermind, Comoros citizen Fazul Abdullah Mohammed, came and went from Somalia. The use of Somalia as a transshipment point for terrorist weapons, and as a temporary safe haven for foreign terrorists conducting attacks against Western targets, constituted a significant evolution in Somalia's role in terrorism.

The use of Somalia as a transshipment point and a short-term safe haven for foreign terrorists resurfaced again in December 2002, when terrorists bombed a Mombasa hotel and attempted to bring down an Israeli charter plane at Mombasa airport. Evidence later emerged that foreign suspects acquired surface-to-air missiles and other explosive material for the attack in Mogadishu, trained there for a month, and then fled into Somalia after the attack to avoid capture.[40] Concerns that Somalia was becoming a safe haven grew in May 2003, when a Yemeni terrorist suspect who had lived and worked in Mogadishu for four years, Suleiman Abdulla Salim Hemed, was apprehended by the Somali militia of Mohamed Dheere, who was working in cooperation with American and Kenyan authorities. In the same month, the US government persuaded Saudi Arabia to close the quasi-government charity al-Harameyn in Somalia on the grounds that it was being used as a front for terrorists.

A foiled terrorist operation in Kenya in June 2003 revealed a new level of Somali involvement in al-Qaeda. The attack on the US embassy in Nairobi, by light aircraft and truck, was not only planned inside Somalia, but also for the first time directly involved Somalis and Somali Kenyans associated with al-Qaeda.

On the basis of these incidents since 1996, the evolution of Somali involvement in terrorism is clear. There is modest but growing Somali complicity in terrorism, principally as a transshipment zone into Kenya, but also as a short-term safe haven for foreign terrorists, and most recently as a source of at least a handful of home-grown al-

Qaeda operatives willing to launch attacks against Western targets. But while counter-terrorism measures must place emphasis on both the real and potential threats emanating from Somalia, the fact remains that its implication in terrorist activities has been modest compared with countries such as Pakistan, Indonesia, Egypt, Yemen or even Kenya. While rising terrorist activity in Somalia is cause for concern, an equally compelling question is why the level of terrorist activity has been so low to date.

The misdiagnosis of collapsed states as safe havens

The fact that Somalia appears to have played a relatively minor role in al-Qaeda operations is in some ways a puzzle. Conventional wisdom holds that collapsed states constitute a safe haven for international terrorists. The logic behind this proposition is, on the surface, entirely reasonable and compelling. Zones of state collapse appear to offer a sanctuary beyond the rule of law, where terrorists can establish bases or staging grounds with little risk of detection. Terrorists will, therefore, naturally prefer the impunity of anarchy to the risks of operating within the reach of a national security and police force.

This logic made it easy for many in the US government and media to short-list Somalia as a site for an expanded war on terrorism following the 11 September bombings. Somalia appeared to have all the ingredients of an ideal safe haven for al-Qaeda. But the environment analysts assumed would be most attractive was, for some reason, not. The case of Somalia suggests that we may have been partially mistaken in our assumptions about the relationship between terrorism and collapsed states. In fact, transnational criminals and terrorists have found zones of complete state collapse like Somalia to be relatively inhospitable territory out of which to operate. There are certainly exceptions – the fiefdoms of drug-lords and radicals in parts of Colombia, for instance. But in general, terrorist networks have instead found safety in weak, corrupted or quasi-states – Pakistan, Yemen, Kenya, the Philippines, Guinea, Indonesia. Terrorist networks, like mafias, appear to flourish where states are governed badly, rather than not at all.

Somalia is less than ideal as a safe haven for al-Qaeda for several reasons. First, in zones of complete state collapse terrorist cells and bases are much more exposed to international counter-terrorist action. Violations of state sovereignty by a US special forces mission would be less problematic (or would even go undetected) where a central government either does not exist, or is unable to extend its authority to large sections of the country. The establishment of an 1,800–strong base at Camp Lemonier in neighbouring Djibouti, designed to provide the US military with what one spokesperson termed the capacity to 'go into an ungoverned area in pursuit of al-Qaida', serves as a reminder of America's ability to launch such counter-terrorist missions.[41] Likewise, in a zone of complete state collapse the US and its allies can contract out the hunt for terrorist suspects to local militias and warlords with few political complications, a practice the US is currently employing in Somalia via the services of several warlords. Mohamed Dheere's militia, for instance, succeeded in tracking and capturing the Yemeni suspect Suleiman Abdalla Salim Hemed in May 2003. Were the US to engage in this kind of bounty-hunting inside the territory of a sovereign state, it would create fierce objections and political complications.

Second, areas of state collapse tend to be inhospitable and dangerous, meaning that few if any foreigners choose to reside there. The fewer the foreigners, the more difficult it is for a foreign terrorist to blend in. The number of non-Somalis resident in Somalia probably numbers only in the hundreds. Those who do live in the country are mainly international aid workers, businessmen, teachers in Islamic schools and spouses. Unless exceptional measures are taken to hide a foreigner in a safe house, a non-Somali's presence is known to all, and is a matter of great interest to local communities. To the extent that secrecy matters to a terrorist cell – and it is safe to presume that it matters a great deal – a collapsed state is not an ideal location. There, terrorists may be beyond the rule of law, but not beyond the purview of curious and suspicious locals. The case of Suleiman Abdulla suggests that a non-Somali terrorist can pose as a legitimate businessman and operate freely for a period, but Abdulla's eventual identification and apprehension also demonstrate how risky that tactic is in a context like Somalia. Likewise, it is possible that a cell of Somali Islamists could provide shelter for a foreign al-Qaeda member in hiding – and rumours circulate in Mogadishu that such safe houses exist – but to remain undetected that individual would be forced to live under virtual house arrest.

Third, the lawlessness of collapsed states such as Somalia significantly increases vulnerability to the most common crimes of chaos – kidnapping, extortion, blackmail and assassination. The same security threats which plague international aid agencies in these areas would also afflict foreign terrorist groups. Ironically, it appears that lawlessness of one type can inhibit, rather than facilitate, lawlessness of another.

Fourth, foreign terrorists would be exceptionally susceptible to betrayal by Somalis eager to reap the rewards of handing over a terrorist suspect to the US. Somali leaders have seized upon the war on terrorism as an opportunity to demonstrate their value to the West as partners, in the expectation that this might translate into tangible benefits – foreign and military aid. Two weeks after the terrorist attacks in 2001, the TNG declared the establishment of a 'national anti-terrorism task force' intended to 'design a comprehensive anti-terrorist national policy'. The argument was that if the West wanted to ensure that no external terrorist cells were operating inside Somalia, it had to support a local authority which could police the country – namely the TNG. Political leaders in Puntland, Somaliland and the Somali Reconciliation and Restoration Council (SRRC, a loose coalition of pro-Ethiopian, anti-TNG factions) all made similar appeals, hoping to parlay American anti-terrorism into foreign aid.[42]

Finally, external actors find zones of endemic state collapse and armed conflict a notoriously difficult environment in which to maintain neutrality. Somalia has been exceptionally challenging on this score. Local contacts and supporters are invariably partisans in local disputes, and the external actor – whether an aid agency or terrorist cell – can quickly become embroiled in those disputes, 'choosing sides' simply by making hiring, rental and contract decisions. Once an external actor is viewed as being 'owned' by a particular clan, it becomes a legitimate target for reprisals by rivals.

By contrast, quasi-states offer a modicum of protection. Governments, however weak, enjoy and fiercely guard their juridical sovereignty, forcing the US and key allies into awkward and not entirely satisfactory partnerships in pursuit of terrorists. The mixed record the US has had with the government of Yemen over investigations into the attack on the USS *Cole* in October 2000 is a case in point. Anti-terrorist joint ventures with governments of quasi-states are cumbersome and often ineffective, since the capacity of such states is often very low. They can also be dangerous, since governments of quasi-states often contain civil servants and military officers with divided loyalties to both the state and the cause.

Information-sharing in such a setting can quickly lead to leaks, failed missions and the danger of compromising informants. Finally, leaders are often exceptionally vulnerable to internal opposition and are as a result unenthusiastic about embracing anti-terrorist actions which might alienate radical groups with whom they have established a modus vivendi. This is an important political factor even in relatively strong states, such as Egypt and Saudi Arabia.

The alternative – simply to violate the sovereignty of a quasi-state in pursuit of individuals or groups suspected of terrorist links – is an option, but one loaded with political complications. Such an operation would create a backlash even in a friendly but weak state (such as Kenya, Yemen or Pakistan), generating a windfall of angry new recruits for al-Qaeda, reinforcing the conviction in some quarters that the real threat is American imperialism, and possibly jeopardising the government in power or forcing it to take anti-American positions for the sake of political survival. A botched operation – one in which innocent locals were killed, or American forces taken hostage – would be enormously difficult to manage if it were conducted without the consent of the government concerned. Although it is easy to disparage the principle of state sovereignty as a legal fiction, its military violation in the pursuit of terrorists would carry a hefty price tag.

A second reason terrorist cells prefer weak states over collapsed ones is that they host a large foreign community – diplomats, aid workers, businesspeople, teachers, tourists, missionaries and partners in mixed marriages, among others. This gives foreign terrorists the ability to move about and mix into the society without arousing immediate attention. In countries like Kenya, where the citizenry is already thoroughly multi-ethnic, this advantage is magnified still further. Large, unpoliced, multi-ethnic cities and slums are especially easy places to dissolve into the crowd. The large foreign presence not only provides cover but also a range of 'soft' Western targets, as Kenya has twice demonstrated. By contrast, Somalia presents a paucity of Western targets.

Third, quasi-states generally feature corrupt security and law-enforcement agencies, but not such high levels of criminality that a terrorist cell is especially vulnerable to lawless behaviour. Bribes to police, border guards and airport officials allow terrorists to circumvent the law even while they enjoy a level of protection from it. In Kenya, even when terrorist suspects have been arrested and incarcerated, corrupt police appear to be bribable: in September 2002, for instance, two suspects in the Mombasa terrorist attacks of September 2002 escaped from custody in March 2003.[43]

Terrorist networks in a region such as East Africa would have a strong and logical preference to work out of Nairobi, Dar es Salaam or even the Ugandan capital Kampala, rather than Somalia. This is precisely what has happened. This does not, however, mean that the world can rest easy about terrorist exploitation of Somalia's anarchy. Areas of state collapse appear to have a niche role to play. Available evidence suggests that they are useful primarily as transit stations, through which the movement of men, money and materiel can be arranged into neighbouring states with little fear of detection. The Horn of Africa is currently awash with unpoliced, cross-border smuggling of small arms, people and goods via Somalia. The use of collapsed states for terrorist transit operations has the advantage of exploiting flourishing smuggling networks (so little suspicion is aroused, and the hiring of trucks and agents is routine) while keeping such involvement in the collapsed state short-term in duration, thereby minimising risks. Local agents need not be members or sympathisers of a terrorist movement; for a fee, virtually any merchant or local warlord will assist in the transit of a shipment, a money transfer or a convoy of people.

Careful monitoring and surveillance of Somalia is an entirely justifiable component of the war on terrorism. But such monitoring should focus primarily on beach ports and cross-border smuggling points rather than on a search for terrorist cells and training camps. It is not what is in these zones of anarchy, but what passes through them, that is of greatest immediate danger. At the same time, the increase in the scope of terrorist activities inside Somalia is likely to continue, especially if global counter-terrorism measures succeed in denying al-Qaeda access to reliable bases elsewhere. Somalia may well become a more active hub of al-Qaeda activities for 'push' rather than 'pull' reasons – because it is the best of a set of bad options for al-Qaeda, not because it is an attractive base.

Conclusion

Policy Implications

Much of the conventional wisdom on the Somali crisis – the nature and scope of its lawlessness, the dynamics of its armed conflicts, the interests of its key political actors in rebuilding a functional state and reviving the rule of law, the agenda and strength of its radical Islamist groups, and the extent to which it is a safe haven for global terrorist networks – is a misreading. This has contributed to flawed and even counterproductive policies in pursuit of national reconciliation, state-building and, more recently, counter-terrorism. This kind of misdiagnosis is not unique to Somalia: it is common to other instances of state collapse, warlordism and 'new wars'. Western policymakers repeatedly view these crises through standard orthodoxies about war and peace, in both their liberal and conservative variants. Analysts such as David Keen have called attention to the costs of the misinterpretations which result, arguing that a more accurate understanding of these conflicts is vital 'for anyone thinking of "policy prescriptions" that might facilitate a lasting peace: A good doctor will need to get some idea of the nature of the disease before rushing to the medicine cabinet to pull out a remedy'.[1]

There are numerous potential explanations for this phenomenon. It can be partially attributed to residual thinking. Policymakers in Western capitals, whose worldview has for decades been shaped by the notion that wars are fought to be won and that a state is essential for the existence of the rule of law, are slow to accept the radical implications of war as a state of 'durable disorder'. Even the inventory of actors is alien – they have no point of reference for interacting with the messy universe of non-state actors in collapsed states. Some observers have gone so far as to imply that this chronic

misreading of 'new wars' is driven by a political culture in the West
that hinders clear thinking about these crises. The politics of genocide
and warlordism, contends Donald Rothchild, 'lies to some extent
beyond the reach of the liberal Western regime'.[2] Moreover, these
assumptions about the nature of war, peace, crime and the rule of law
are built into 'post-conflict reconstruction' programmes, crystallised
into templates which leave very little room for reinterpretation.
Challenging a key premise about the nature of these crises risks
undermining the entire corpus of standard responses to armed
conflict and collapsed government – from diplomatic mediation to
foreign assistance programmes to peacekeeping. Not surprisingly,
such interpretations of collapsed states and warlordism meet with
institutional resistance. The result can be diplomatic and state-
building approaches in some collapsed states akin to rearranging
deckchairs on the *Titanic*.

Whether a function of cultural blinkers, residual thinking, poor
information, inflexible bureaucratic templates in the UN or simply
sloppy analysis, the product of the misreading of these crises is
misguided policy. Somalia has been no exception. The logic which
springs from the prevailing misdiagnosis of Somalia and its policy
implications can be summarised as follows: Somalia's collapsed state
constitutes a threat to global security because it provides a safe haven
for terrorists. To prevent terrorists from exploiting Somalia, an
effective law-enforcement capacity must be built up. Such a capacity
requires a revived central state. National reconciliation efforts must
therefore produce an accord which establishes a national government.

The analysis presented in this paper exposes numerous
problems with this line of reasoning and the policies it has produced.
First, it has demonstrated that the lack of an implemented peace and a
revived central state is precisely the outcome which key Somali
political actors desire. Convening peace conferences with
constituencies who prefer an ongoing state of collapse, lawlessness
and conflict is an exercise in futility. The repeated failure of these peace
initiatives is not therefore simply the result of diplomatic
incompetence or myopic Somali leadership; it is a result which at least
some Somali political actors and their external patrons have come to
the table determined to produce.

Second, even if a peace accord is successfully brokered in
Somalia and results in a power-sharing agreement which revives a

central government – a scenario which the trend analysis in this paper anticipates, as the interests of key Somali constituencies gradually shift – the government which emerges will be little more than a 'paper state' designed to attract foreign aid and embassies, but not necessarily to govern. Too many powerful economic actors profit from the absence of a functional central authority; they may eventually be willing to risk the revival of a state, but only if it is thoroughly defanged. The result would be a government which would enjoy the perquisites of a sovereign state – mainly foreign aid – without the capacity or inclination to impose the rule of law. Far from monitoring and apprehending terrorist cells, such a paper state could conceivably render Somalia more attractive to terrorists. Somalia is by some measures a less permissive environment for terrorists as a collapsed state than it would be as a weak and ineffective one.

The conventional and entirely understandable response to this concern is to propose 'capacity-building' projects designed to strengthen local law enforcement, so that the failed state (or subnational administration) can quickly begin effectively policing the population. This approach has gained new appeal since 11 September, the point at which nation-building was 'securitised' and capacity-building became a matter of urgency in the war on terrorism. A key component of that war is depriving terrorists of a base of operations. This 'draining the swamp' strategy necessarily involves a concerted effort to strengthen the law-enforcement capacity of weak and failed states such as Somalia.

In theory, this seems self-evident. In practice, the analysis presented in this paper points to a number of serious problems with the enterprise of rebuilding functional governments in collapsed states like Somalia with the expectation that they will quickly assume a role as reliable law-enforcement partners in the war on terrorism. First, the many local interests in Somalia which do not share the same enthusiasm for a formal law-enforcement capacity will quietly undermine such projects (while gladly taking the funding). Second, building an effective, formal law-enforcement capacity in Somalia is a massive task, far greater than the foreign aid which the country has attracted to date. This would not constitute a *revival* of pre-existing law-enforcement structures; rather, it would involve developing this capacity in Somalia for the very first time. It would also entail a transformation of the relationship between state and society.

The central Somali state has never been the source of the rule of law, but has instead been a catalyst for criminality, violence and communal tensions. The lawful and peaceful conditions which have obtained in parts of Somalia are the result of a social contract and traditional conflict-management mechanisms. In the future, the central state in Somalia may well come to play a vital role in ensuring the rule of law, but that will involve a profound political change, which will not be achieved via police training sessions on human rights.

Third, and perhaps most importantly, this analysis highlights a paradox when nation-building is pursued as a strategy in the war on terror. The task of rebuilding the capacity of a collapsed state like Somalia to govern and police effectively is enormous, and even in the best of situations can require a decade or two of sustained assistance. The long stretch of time which passes between state collapse and effectively rebuilt government constitutes a dangerous transitional stage, a period when the government on the receiving end of nation-building efforts is weak, vulnerable, but sovereign – in other words, a quasi-state. Hence the security paradox of nation-building: the very success of post-conflict reconstruction in a collapsed state will produce a temporary political situation in which terrorist networks appear to thrive.

This is not a new idea: Samuel Huntington argued over three decades ago that while both traditional and modern polities are stable, political instability is endemic in countries in transition from traditional to modern society.[3] If this same transitional dynamic is true in nation-building and public security, then we can expect the current sites of nation-building initiatives to become more, not less, dangerous as terrorist safe havens in the short term. This outcome is possible even if post-conflict reconstruction initiatives are strategically coherent, vigorous, seamlessly coordinated and flawlessly executed. It is virtually certain if current nation-building systems and practices are left in place, delivering the half-way measures which produce half-way, quasi-states.

At the heart of the security dilemma of nation-building in countries like Somalia lie two propositions, both of which are disquietingly true. The first identifies collapsed states as a security threat in the war on terrorism. The second argues that nation-building as currently conceived and executed is a fool's errand. This dilemma is at the heart of the Bush administration's perplexing ambivalence about post-war reconstruction in Afghanistan.

There are only a few potential policy responses to this impasse. None is ideal; the phenomenon of collapsed states and the security concerns they raise present only bad options. One approach is to quietly abandon the nation-building enterprise in places like Somalia as pointless and accept that the war on terrorism will be reactive, not preventive – executed as a protracted military and counter-terrorist operation against threats which thrive in swamps we have opted not to try to drain. Somalia and comparable crises of state collapse will be contained and closely monitored, but not resolved. There are obvious costs and shortcomings with this approach, not least of which is that it condemns the war on terror to a battle in perpetuity. But it has attractive virtues too. It frees Western states from the messy, unsatisfying, risky and long-term task of reviving failed states; and, by emphasising military responses, it plays to the strengths of the US. It is thus entirely plausible that this approach will win favour in American circles if and when frustration with nation-building in places like Afghanistan and Iraq hits critical mass. A comment by US Senator Joseph Biden hints at this possibility: 'Some of these guys [in DoD] don't go for nation-building. They think it's cheaper to just go back in and empty the swamp again if you have to'.[4] Current US practice in Somalia – bounty-hunting arrangements with local warlords to seek out foreign terrorist suspects – falls clearly within the scope of this approach.

It is equally plausible that nation-building in Somalia and elsewhere will continue with only incremental reform, despite the fact that it is clearly failing. The UN's 'light-footprint' approach in Afghanistan is an outstanding example of such a package – well-intentioned and reasonable, but only addressing one portion (the questions of sustainability and ownership) of a much larger set of problems in post-conflict reconstruction. UN agencies, and donor states, are notoriously resistant to changing their policies, and may prefer standard operating procedures regardless of their effectiveness. This option also has the political attraction of demonstrating that external states are 'doing something' in the face of public or diplomatic pressure to act.

The more draconian solution to the security dilemma of collapsed states is some form of trusteeship. This entails the concerned external party (presumably the UN, the US, NATO, the EU or another regional organisation) assuming direct control of law enforcement and the surveillance of criminal or terrorist activity, while allowing the state in receivership gradually to build up its capacity to govern. Trusteeship-type solutions to failed states are not popular either in the West (where the cost is viewed as too high and the commitment too long) or in the developing world (where it is viewed with great suspicion as a pretext for imperialism, particularly in the aftermath of the US occupation and administration of Iraq). Yet trusteeship, which not long ago was essentially a relic of UN history, has experienced a small revival in recent years, first with the UN operation in Cambodia, then with the UN trusteeships in East Timor and Kosovo. The ultimate fate of the interim governing authority in occupied Iraq will be the real test of quasi-trusteeship solutions to the security dilemma of collapsed states.

Whether some variation on trusteeship is a good policy option vis-à-vis collapsed states is a debate which cannot be resolved here. But what is clear is that such a costly and controversial approach will, if it is adopted at all, almost certainly be limited to a handful of the most strategically important collapsed states. For Somalia, this is an unlikely option, though many leading Somali political figures insist that it is the only solution to the Somali impasse.[5] Somalia is too poor and marginal, and the legacy of the failed UNOSOM mission too poisonous. Discussions of external engagement will remain cautious and minimalist for years to come.

This inventory of policy options may appear bleak. But the analysis presented in this paper, while sobering, is not pessimistic. Indeed, two of its central themes – that the dynamics of collapsed government, lawlessness and armed conflict in Somalia have changed considerably over the past decade, and that the evolving interests of key Somali constituencies are driving these changes – are hopeful. While a formal and effective central government may be a distant dream, other forces are at play which have an interest in improving human development, lawfulness, conflict management and the capacity to monitor and prevent terrorist infiltration, even in the absence of a central state.

External actors can either promote or obstruct this process. Here is where a diplomatic equivalent of the humanitarian principle of 'do no harm' is appropriate. Often, external forays into Somali national reconciliation only reinforce the worst instincts of the nation's political and economic elite, by reinforcing a kind of 'cargo cult' mentality: massive foreign aid will soon flow again to those clever enough to convince foreigners that they control what passes for a sovereign state. This is precisely what fuels so much conflict whenever international interlocutors convene a national reconciliation conference.

This 'do no harm' admonition holds true as well for ongoing policy discussions on Somaliland. Somaliland's impressive success in maintaining peace and stability, its economic recovery, and its steps toward multi-party democracy have earned it a growing number of admirers in the external community. Somaliland's accomplishments stand in sharp contrast to the ongoing crisis in southern Somalia, and have raised the question in some quarters as to whether the international community ought not provide more direct support, and perhaps even diplomatic recognition, to Somaliland.[6] Among the many arguments in favour of recognition of Somaliland is the claim that shoring up an island of political stability in a troubled region makes sense from both a regional and global security perspective. But while policymakers in the West consider some sort of diplomatic recognition for Somaliland (including gestures which fall short of outright acceptance of Somaliland's secession), care must be taken to insure that whatever recognition is extended helps to reinforce, not undermine, Somaliland's political successes. Specifically, recognition must not give the Somaliland leadership the means to strengthen the executive branch against the legislature; postpone or manipulate Somaliland's fragile movements towards multi-party democratisation; derail plans for political decentralisation; deflect demands for greater government accountability and transparency; or seek a military solution to the dangerous showdown between Somaliland and Puntland over the contested regions of Sool and Sanaag. Instead, recognition must come with conditions attached which press the Hargeisa administration for better governance.

Rather than repeatedly embracing processes which bring out the worst in the Somali polity (and thereby reinforce external stereotypes about Somalia), a better tactic would be to focus on playing to Somalia's strengths, working with rather than against the prevailing political currents and trends in the country. Somalia's robust entrepreneurship, for instance, has the potential to be either destructive or beneficial. Strategies which engage the Somali commercial elite, which build incentives into cooperative relations with the West rather than simply threatening Somali businesses with punitive measures should they have any dealings with radical Islamists, would help to promote economic recovery while tapping into a well-informed network of businesspeople to help monitor and prevent terrorist activities. Cooperative relations with effective local and regional authorities, including clan elders, would reinforce the message that political legitimacy in Somalia is earned by governing and governing well, not simply by attending peace conferences. Until Somalia's central government is revived, the outside world would advance its own interests and those of the Somali people by learning to deal with stateless Somalia on its own terms, not by insisting that Somali representatives remake themselves in our likeness. Engaging with Somalis on their own terms also means recognising the wide diversity of positions on Islamist politics in Somalia, and considering the possibility of opening quiet, informal dialogue with al-Islah, currently the most robust social movement in Somalia. There can be little margin of error in assessing and responding to the many faces of political Islam in Somalia and the Horn of Africa. A 'boilerplate' approach which downplays or looks past these differences by viewing political Islam as monolithic is likely to produce policies which worsen rather than improve Western security concerns in the region.

Notes

Introduction

1. Michael Ignatieff has called this 'the indignation machine of the modern media'. See 'Why Are We in Iraq? (And Liberia? And Afghanistan?)', *New York Times Magazine*, 7 September 2003, http://www.nytimes.com/2003/09/07/magazine/07INTERVENTION.html.

2. Detailed exploration of the tensions between the 'right to intervene' and the principle of state sovereignty is provided in International Commission on Intervention and State Sovereignty (ICISS), *The Responsibility to Protect: Report of the International Commission on Intervention and State Sovereignty* (Ottawa: International Development Research Centre, 2001).

3. The prospects for the securitisation of complex emergencies prior to 9/11 are assessed in Ken Menkhaus, 'Complex Emergencies, Humanitarianism, and National Security', *National Security Studies Quarterly*, vol. 4, no. 4, Autumn 1998, pp. 53-61.

4. John J. Hamre and Gordon R. Sullivan, 'Toward Postconflict Reconstruction', *Washington Quarterly*, vol. 25, no. 4, Autumn 2002, p. 85.

5. The terms 'lawlessness' and 'lawfulness' are used here not in their strict, formal sense, which would be meaningless given the absence in Somalia of a sovereign state authority to enforce the law. They are meant instead to convey the extent to which common criminal behaviour (murder, robbery, extortion, kidnapping) is or is not taking place. Since Somali society possesses a long tradition of customary law brokered between clans and enforced by clan elders, the notion of 'lawless' or 'criminal' behaviour occurring in a context of state collapse is not as absurd as it might first appear.

6. The literature on war economies and 'resource wars' is now quite large. For a sample of this research, see Mats Berdal and David Malone (eds), *Greed and Grievance: Economic Agendas in Civil Wars* (Boulder, CO: Lynne Rienner Publishers, 2000); David Keen, *The Economic Functions of Violence in Civil Wars*, Adelphi Paper 320 (Oxford: Oxford University Press for the IISS, 1998); William Reno, *Warlord Politics and African States* (Boulder, CO: Lynne Rienner Publishers, 2000); Mark Duffield, 'The Political Economy of Internal War: Asset Transfer, Complex

Emergencies, and International Aid', in Joanna Macrae, Anthony Zwi and Hugo Slim (eds), *War and Hunger: Rethinking International Responses to Complex Emergencies* (London: Zed Books, 1996), pp. 50-69; Paul Collier, *Breaking the Poverty Trap: Civil War and Development Policy* (Washington DC: World Bank, 2003); and Paul Collier and Anke Hoeffler, 'Greed and Grievance in Civil Wars', World Bank Policy Research Paper WPS2355, 2000, http://www.worldbank.org/research/conflict.

[7] This conclusion supports the thesis on risk-aversion in contemporary civil wars developed by Charles King in *Ending Civil Wars, Adelphi Paper 308* (Oxford: Oxford University Press for the IISS, 1997).

Chapter 1

[1] One study, based on the findings of the Harvard University Failed States Project, attempts to distinguish between failed states and collapsed states; see Robert Rotberg (ed.), *State Failure and State Weakness in a Time of Terror* (Washington DC: Brookings Institution Press, 2003), pp. 5–10.

[2] The State Failure Task Force, a CIA-sponsored research project established in 1994 to explore causes of state failure, identified 127 cases between 1955 and 1996. The project's working definition of state failure was instances when 'the institutions of the state were so weakened that they could no longer maintain authority or political order beyond the capital city, and sometimes not even there. [Cases of state failure] are all part of a syndrome of serious political crisis which, in the extreme case, leads to the collapse of governance'. See Daniel C. Esty, Jack A. Goldstone, Ted Robert Gurr, *et al.*, 'State Failure Task Force Report: Phase II', in *Environmental Change and Security Report* (Washington DC: Wilson Center, 2000), http://wwics.si.edu/index.cfm?topic_id=1413&fuseaction=topics.publications&group_id=6653.

[3] Christopher Clapham, *Africa and the International System: The Politics of State Survival* (Cambridge: Cambridge University Press, 1996), p. 22.

[4] Ken Menkhaus, 'International Peacebuilding and the Dynamics of Local and National Peacebuilding in Somalia', in Walter Clarke and Jeffrey Herbst (eds), *Learning from Somalia: The Lessons of Armed Humanitarian Intervention* (Boulder, CO: Westview Press, 1997), p. 58.

[5] This is a controversial assertion in diplomatic circles, but even UN reports to the Security Council, which are normally purged of any politically sensitive statements, have acknowledged that preparations for the Eldoret peace process set in motion intense political jockeying between rival groups in places like Mogadishu, and in some cases led to bloodshed. See UN Security Council, *Report of the Secretary-General on the Situation in Somalia* (New York: United Nations, 21 February 2002), para. 6; and UN Security Council, *Report of the Team of Experts Appointed Pursuant to Security Council Resolution 1407 (2002), Paragraph 1, Concerning Somalia* (New York: United Nations, 3 July 2002), paras 28, 32.

[6] International Crisis Group, 'A Blueprint for Peace in Somalia', ICG Africa Report 59 (Mogadishu/Brussels: ICG, 6 March 2003), http://www.crisisweb.org, p. 6.

[7] Ken Menkhaus, 'Getting Out Versus Getting Through: US and UN Policies in Somalia', *Middle East Policy*, vol. 3, no. 1, 1994, p. 150.

8   The IGAD-sponsored Somalia peace talks in 2002–2003 were initially held in Eldoret in Kenya, and were known throughout 2002 as the Eldoret talks. In early 2003, the site of the talks was moved to Mbagathi, on the outskirts of Nairobi, and since that time have been referred to as the Mbagathi talks. In this study, the terms 'Eldoret talks' and 'Mbagathi talks' refer to the same IGAD-sponsored process.

9   Population figures for Somalia are unknown and estimates must be treated with caution. The two million figure provided here is drawn from International Crisis Group, 'Somaliland: Democratisation and Its Discontents', ICG Africa Report 66 (Nairobi: Brussels: ICG, 28 July 2003), http://www.crisisweb.org, p. 2.

10 The contested regions of Sool and Sanaag (home of the Dolbahante/Harti and Warsengeli/Harti clans) have for several years been a source of tension between Puntland and Somaliland, but not outright armed conflict. Somaliland claims the regions based on their inclusion in colonial British Somaliland, a border which is the legal basis for Somaliland's claim of independence. Puntland claims the areas based on the fact that the Harti clan resides in the two regions, invoking a sort of 'right of lineage self-determination' for its clan. Each administration has named its own governor to the two regions, creating an odd situation where two governors live in the same town. Since neither actually governs, the situation is less problematic than it would seem. Still, in late 2002 armed clashes erupted in the regional capital of Las Anod which drew forces from both Somaliland and Puntland into the fray. In early 2004, Puntland moved militia into Las Anod, prompting a troop build-up by Somaliland and a tense stand-off in the region.

11 Ken Menkhaus, *Hiran Region*, United Nations Development Office for Somalia (UNDOS) Studies on Governance Series no. 7 (Nairobi: UNDOS, December 1999).

12 Matt Bryden, 'New Hope for Somalia? The Building Block Approach', *Review of African Political Economy*, vol. 26, no. 79, March 1999, pp. 134–140.

13 ICG, 'A Blueprint for Peace', p. 8.

14 The term 'minority' is politically loaded in Somalia. In its more general usage, it refers to members of 'low-caste' lineages, including and perhaps especially 'hard-hairs' (*jereer*), who are physically distinct from ethnic Somalis; some are descendents of Bantu-speaking slaves from East Africa. This paragraph uses the term 'minority' in the strictly numerical sense – a clan which is only 20% of the population in one district is a minority there, though it may be the majority lineage in the adjacent district.

15 The use of expressions involving the word 'ethnic' is problematic in the Somali context; some anthropologists argue that, technically, Somalis constitute a single ethnic group, and that the term 'ethnic group' and 'clan' should not be used interchangeably. This paper uses the word 'ethnic' in the most general sense. See I. M. Lewis, 'A Response from Professor I. M. Lewis', *Journal of the Anglo-Somali Society*, no. 32, Autumn 2002, p. 19.

16 Ken Menkhaus and John Prendergast, 'Governance and Economic Survival in Post-Intervention Somalia', *CSIS Africa Notes*, no. 172, May 1995.

17 The author conducted research on local governance for the UN Development Office for Somalia in 1998 in five regions of southern

Somalia – a summary report of trends in Somali local governance based on that research is available in Ken Menkhaus, *Political and Security Assessment of Southern Somalia: Implications for Emergency Response* (Nairobi: UNDOS, 11 December 1998).

[18] Andre Le Sage, 'Prospects for Al Itihad and Islamist Radicalism in Somalia', *Review of African Political Economy*, vol. 28, no. 89, September 2001, pp. 472–77; and Ken Menkhaus, 'Political Islam in Somalia', *Middle East Policy*, vol. 9, no. 1, March 2002, p. 116.

[19] International Crisis Group, 'Somalia: Combating Terrorism in a Failed State', ICG Africa Report 45 (Brussels/Washington: ICG, May 2002), http://www.crisisweb.org.

[20] Robert Kaplan, 'The Coming Anarchy', *The Atlantic Monthly*, vol. 273, no. 2, February 1994, pp. 44–76.

[21] A bleak summary of the deteriorating state of security in Somalia in 2002 is provided by the UN Security Council, *Report of the Secretary-General on the Situation in Somalia* (New York: United Nations, 25 October 2002) (S/20021201), paras 7–17.

[22] Matt Bryden, 'Security Challenges and the International Dimensions of the Somali Crisis', *Journal of Conflict Studies*, vol. 22, no. 2, Autumn 2003.

[23] The Darood clan family actually split into several different factions in 1991, but for the sake of simplicity those splits are not treated here.

[24] Looting in southern Somalia set new and appalling standards for wartime banditry. Pillaging was not limited to the personal belongings of villagers and townspeople (including the metal sheets serving as the roofs of their homes): the entire infrastructure – even underground waterpipes and telephone lines – was dismantled and sold as scrap metal in Kenya. One leading Somali political and financial figure was implicated in the most outrageous instance of criminal looting – the dismantling of the $225 million Juba Sugar Project factory, which reportedly fetched one million dollars as scrap.

[25] One close observer of the fighting in Mogadishu reports that the average cost of a full-scale armed clash by a militia is about $4,000 an hour in ammunition, a steep price which few warlords are capable of sustaining; hence it is unusual for armed clashes to last more than a few hours.

[26] One of the puzzling aspects of Somali warlordism is why so few of these militia leaders had the foresight to develop their own sustainable sources of funding. Most are forced to ask for support from businessmen and elders in their clans, or to rely on the sporadic support of an external state. One example of warlord entrepreneurship is the Mogadishu-based militia leader Mohamed Qanyare, who has a diversified portfolio of business interests ranging from fishing to a private airstrip in the Deynile neighbourhood. This has afforded him the capacity to pay militia consistently and remain independent of external patrons, clan elders and businessmen, and has meant that he has come to enjoy a position of strength relative to less business-savvy warlords.

[27] United Nations Office for the Coordination of Humanitarian Affairs, *Somalia Humanitarian Situation Report*, Nairobi, 30 July 2003, pp. 5–6.

[28] In some instances, kinsmen lose patience with the costs of criminality by a member of their *diya* (blood-compensation) group and have the individual arrested or executed. Vigilante justice is also associated with

neighbourhood security groups
and with the militia of private
businessmen, who occasionally
hunt down criminal gangs. One
posse killed six professional
criminals in an attack outside
Mogadishu in November 2002
(personal correspondence,
November 2002).

29 An excellent journalistic piece on
the interests entangled in
kidnapping in Somalia is Alexis
Masciarelli, 'Somalia's
Kidnapping Industry', BBC news
website, 24 May 2002,
http://news.bbc.co.uk/2/hi/afric
a/2005567.stm.

30 Ken Menkhaus, 'Somalia: Next Up
in the War on Terrorism?', *CSIS
Africa Notes*, no. 6, January 2002,
http://www.csis.org/ANotes/ind
ex.htm.

Chapter 2

1 The external actors supporting the
current peace talks in Kenya have
consciously sought to shape these
interests in state-building, mainly
via threats of sanctions against
recalcitrant warlords if they fail to
cooperate. Mike Crawley, 'Somalia
Restarts Search for Way to End 11
Years of War and Chaos', *Christian
Science Monitor*, 16 October 2002,
accessed via ReliefWeb at
http://www.reliefweb.int/w/
rwb.nsf

2 The NSC is primarily a Hawiye-
dominated alliance, but it
includes non-Hawiye politicians
as well. Principals in the group
include Musa Sude, Osman Atto,
Barre Hirale (head of the Jubba
Valley Alliance), Indha Adde (an
emerging strongman in the Lower
Shabelle), Mohamed Habsade
(RRA-Baidoa) and Jama Ali Jama
(rival to Puntland leader
Abdullahi Yusuf).

3 Catherine Bestemen and Lee V.
Cassanelli (eds), *The Struggle for
Land in Southern Somalia: The War
Behind the War* (Boulder, CO:

Westview Press, 1996).

4 Africa Watch, *Somalia: A
Government at War with Its Own
People* (London, New York and
Washington DC: Africa Watch,
January 1990), p. 43.

5 It should be noted that some
individuals are both warlord and
businessman.

6 Roland Marchal has argued this
point with regard to the business
class and its import of counterfeit
currency. See Marchal's chapter in
UNDP, *Somalia Human
Development Report 2001* (Nairobi:
UNDP, 2001). The hyperinflation
created by illegal imports of
counterfeit currency by
businessmen with close ties to the
TNG prompted riots in
Mogadishu in April 2001 and
badly eroded public support for
the TNG.

7 This appeared to be a major factor
in the undermining of what was
for a time a highly effective local
sharia court system in Beled Weyn
(Hiran region) in the late 1990s.
There, the 'governor' of the
region, a warlord notorious in aid
agency circles for having overseen
the looting of the WFP warehouse
in 1993, used his sub-clan's unruly
gunmen to challenge and
eventually bring down a court
system which had enjoyed
widespread popular support and
which had delivered much more
by way of good governance than
the governor could countenance.
See Menkhaus, *Hiran* Region,
chapter 4.

8 Andre Le Sage, 'Somalia:
Sovereign Disguise for a
Mogadishu Mafia', *Review of
African Political Economy*, vol. 29,
no. 91, March 2002, p. 132.

9 UN Integrated Regional
Information Network (IRIN),
'Somalia: Scandal Hits
Transitional Government',
Reliefweb, 29 June 2001,
www.reliefweb.org.

10 An important distinction needs to

be drawn between different categories of businessmen in Mogadishu. A small group – perhaps as few as three wealthy individuals – appear to have been wholly committed to the TNG, for political, business and clan reasons. A second category supported the TNG tactically, viewing their financial contributions as venture capital which they expected to recoup once foreign aid flowed to the TNG. A third group of businessmen supported the TNG only because they were forced to do so by social pressures, but were from the start much less enthusiastic about the venture than media reports suggested at the time.
[11] Author's fieldwork, June–August 2002.

Chapter 3

[1] J. Brian Atwood, 'Suddenly, Chaos', *Washington Post*, 31 July 1994.
[2] Bernard Finel, 'What is Security? Why the Debate Matters', *National Security Studies Quarterly*, vol. 4, no. 4, Autumn 1998, pp. 2–7.
[3] Menkhaus, 'Complex Emergencies, Humanitarianism, and National Security', p. 57.
[4] This is mainly via natural (beach) ports to the north and south of Mogadishu. In recent times, the all-weather seaport of Kismayo has also been used for this transit trade.
[5] The transit trade through Somalia into Kenya is documented in detail in Ken Menkhaus, *Gedo Region*, UNDOS Studies on Governance Series no. 5 (Nairobi: UNDOS, December 1999). See also UNDP, *Somalia Human Development Report 2001*, pp. 93–96.
[6] Robert Muggah and Eric Berman, *Humanitarianism Under Threat: The Humanitarian Impacts of Small Arms and Light Weapons*, Special

Report no. 1 (Geneva: Small Arms Survey, July 2001), p. 10.
[7] Human Rights Watch, *Playing with Fire: Weapons Proliferation, Political Violence, and Human Rights in Kenya* (New York: Human Rights Watch, May 2002).
[8] Human Rights Watch, *Hidden in Plain View: Refugees without Protection in Nairobi and Kampala* (New York: Human Rights Watch, November 2002); Dauti Kahara, 'Proliferation of Small Arms and Insecurity', East African Standard, 3 February 2003.
[9] UNDP, *Somalia Human Development Report 2001*, p. 98.
[10] Less than 30% of Somalis have access to clean drinking water. *Ibid.*, p. 82.
[11] WHO's polio-vaccination campaign in Somalia met with serious obstacles when militiamen insisted that they be hired as the local medical technicians administering the vaccinations despite their lack of training; security incidents occurred when these demands were not met. Author's fieldnotes, 1998.
[12] Current estimates of the rate of HIV infection in the Somali population are around 1%, one of the lowest in Africa, but many observers worry that the figure could be much higher on the assumption that HIV/AIDS cases are underreported. See UNDP, *Somalia Human Development Report 2001*, p. 80.
[13] *Ibid.*, p. 105.
[14] This has primarily been an issue for states with relatively generous welfare and asylum policies. There is a marked difference in the Somali communities congregating in welfare states and those which are attracted to states with no such safety net. Somalis in the US, for instance, face very few problems with the broader community, as most of them have two or even three jobs. Those

gravitating towards states with generous welfare policies, such as Canada and Sweden, are as a group less inclined to seek work. In fairness to the Somali diaspora as a whole, the vast majority are both willing and able to work in their host countries; only a fraction of the entire group creates problems by abusing welfare and asylum laws.

[15] DNA testing makes this particular form of fraud more difficult.

[16] 'Pirate Warning for Somalia's Coastline', BBC website, 30 January 2003, http://www.bbc.co.uk/2/hi/business/2709339.stm.

[17] Roland Marchal, *Islamic Political Dynamics in the Somali Civil War* (Paris: CERI, 2001), p. 9.

[18] At a conference in November 1990, the author presented a paper considering an Islamist regime in Somalia as one of six possible scenarios for post-Barre Somalia; though it was deemed very unlikely as an outcome, its inclusion in the scenario-building exercise provoked considerable objections and even laughter in the mainly Somali audience.

[19] This assessment of Islamic rule in Luuq is derived from fieldwork the author conducted there in 1998, published in Menkhaus, *Gedo Region*.

[20] AMREF, 'Annual Report of the Luuq District Health Programme', Nairobi, 1994.

[21] Roland Marchal, 'An Overall View on the Political Situation in Gedo', unpublished report, 1996.

[22] Interview, October 1998.

[23] Ken Menkhaus, 'Somalia: A Situation Analysis and Trend Assessment', Writenet Paper (Geneva: UNHCR, Protection Information Section, Department of International Protection, August 2003), p. 13.

[24] A strong case for this position is made by Le Sage in 'Prospects for Al Itihad', pp. 472–77.

[25] UN-IRIN, 'Somalia: Aydiid Accuses TNG of Terrorist Links', 26 September 2001, http://www.irinnews.org.

[26] See Le Sage, 'Prospects for Al-Itihad'.

[27] Because of the attacks of 1996, the entire AIAI organisation has been designated a terrorist group by the US Department of State.

[28] Andre Le Sage and Ken Menkhaus, 'The Rise of Islamic Charities in Somalia', paper delivered at the International Studies Association annual conference, Montreal Canada, 17–20 March 2004 (forthcoming).

[29] Bryden, 'Security Challenges and the International Dimensions of the Somali Crisis'.

[30] Numerous security incidents against Western aid agencies inside Somalia have implicated Islamists, but they are usually the result of local disputes. The 2003 incident in which Somalis were directly implicated was the foiled attack against the US embassy in Nairobi.

[31] Chris Tomlinson, 'Somali Network Aids Hunt for Terrorists', *Boston Globe*, 6 November 2003.

[32] Thomas Ricks, 'Allies Step Up Somalia Watch; US Aims to Keep Al Qaeda at Bay', *Washington Post*, 4 January 2002.

[33] Quoted in 'Somalia "Most Likely to Be Next Base" for Al Qaeda', *Straits Times*, 1 December 2001.

[34] Ken Menkhaus, 'Remittance Companies and Money Transfers in Somalia', unpublished paper, October 2001; Roland Marchal, 'The Outcome of US Decision on al-Barakaat', unpublished paper for the European Commission, January 2002; and Mark Bradbury, 'Somalia: The Aftermath of September 11th and the War on Terrorism', unpublished report for Oxfam GB, February 2002, pp. 19–30.

[35] Quoted in Steve Vogel and Karl

Vick, 'Team in Somalia May Be Planning US Strikes', *Washington Post*, 11 December 2001.

36 Quoted in 'Somalia "Most Likely to Be Next Base" for Al Qaeda'.

37 Quoted in *Washington Times*, 9 January 2002, p. A1.

38 A detailed and strident presentation of the Ethiopian view on Al-Ittihad is provided in Tadesse, *Al-Ittihad*.

39 By a quirk of fate, the movie 'Black Hawk Down', with its nightmare scenes of American forces pinned down in urban warfare in Mogadishu, came out just as options for an operation inside Somalia were under discussion.

40 United Nations Security Council, *Report of the Panel of Experts on Somalia Pursuant to Security Council Resolution 1474 (2003)*, S/2003/1035, 4 November 2003, pp. 27–32.

41 'More Troops Sent to Horn of Africa', *New York Times*, 11 August 2002, http://www.nyt.com.

42 Menkhaus, 'Political Islam in Somalia', p. 121.

43 Catherine Bond, 'Source: Kenya Bomb Suspects Flee', CNN.com, 28 March 2003.

Conclusion

1 David Keen, 'Incentives and Disincentives for Violence', in Berdal and Malone (eds), *Greed and Grievance*, p. 20.

2 Donald Rothchild, 'The United States and Africa: Power with Limited Influence', in Robert Lieber (ed.), *Eagle Rules? Foreign Policy and American Primacy in the Twenty-First Century* (Upper Saddle River, NJ: Prentice Hall, 2001), p. 216.

3 Samuel Huntington, *Political Order in Changing Societies* (New Haven, CT: Yale University Press, 1968).

4 Quoted in Bill Keller, 'The Question of American Power', *International Herald Tribune*, 10 February 2003.

5 The prevalence of this sentiment among Somali political elites and intellectuals is remarkable – they are quick to invoke East Timor and Kosovo as evidence that the world 'must' do the same for Somalia.

6 See for example International Crisis Group, 'Somaliland: Democratisation and its Discontents'; Jeffrey Herbst, 'Somaliland Deserves a Closer Look', *Washington Post* 2 January 2004; Mark Bradbury, Adan Yusuf Abokor, and Haroon Ahmed Yusuf, 'Somaliland: Choosing Politics over Violence', *Review of African Political Economy* no. 97 2003, pp. 455–478; David Shinn, 'Somaliland: The Little Country that Could', *CSIS Africa Notes*, no 9, 2002. For a rejoinder, see Ahmed I. Samatar and Abdi I. Samatar, 'The International Crisis Group Report on Somaliland: An Alternative Somali Response', unpublished paper, 13 August 2003.